Acclaim for *Peter Strickland*

"Capt. Peter Strickland owes much to author Stephen H. Grant."—Library of Congress

"Grant's careful blending of historical hindsight with Strickland's own words brings enormous value to our understanding of U.S. diplomacy."—*Foreign Service Journal*

"This book offers a vivid picture of the unique career of a New Englander who was a pioneer in the diplomatic field in French West Africa."—*The Day*, New London, Conn.

"[This] interesting and informative book on a little known connection between this area and the West African country of Senegal . . . opens a window to a neglected aspect of trade in the nineteenth century."—*New London County Historical Society Newsletter*

"What began with the purchase of an envelope on eBay by a man interested in old postcards turned into six years of research culminating in an intriguing new book."—*The Resident*, Stonington, Conn.

"Stephen Grant has written a wonderfully readable account of an exceptional personality."—Eunice Charles

"This is a great new historical source for Senegal, and for 19th century American shipping, trade, and foreign relations."—L. Rebecca Johnson Melvin, University of Delaware Library

"An entertaining, lively read. I do not remember reading anything that brings to life so well this period and the reality of living both in West Africa and in New England."
—Arthur M. Fell

"[Strickland's] career as consul is of interest to historians of Africa in its insights into late nineteenth-century commerce along the coast from Senegal to Sierra Leone and the impact upon the United States' role of the onset of French colonialism. Through his consular dispatches, correspondence, and a journal spanning twenty-five years, he documents the primary imports and exports of Senegal to the U.S., but also the business and social relations among those serving European and American interests from Gorée and Dakar."—Roberta Ann Dunbar

"Stephen Grant's biography is a little gem. The preface tells of the author's search for his subject and reads with the pace and surprise of a treasure hunt. Grant has a special gift for writing history, perhaps especially biography. His eye for detail also sees his subject in the round and in all the colors of his time and setting."—Sam S. Rea

"Grant not only tells a good tale, but he has made an excellent use of a significant trove of historical materials in doing so, conducting extensive research on two continents, examining volumes of archival records and poring over Strickland's six decades of personal journals."—Nina Robbins

"Stephen Grant has done a masterful job of weaving the strands and evidence of a multitalented individual's life into a coherent collage with his biography of the seafaring entrepreneur Peter Strickland. The man had such a mixed life of professional success and unceasing personal tragedy. I thought about life in the mid-1800s: no cars, no planes, and less than luxurious ship conditions. I can't blame his wife for retreating. Life as a whole was incredibly challenging in those days that Grant has written about in such an interesting way."—Mary-Charlotte Shealy

Peter Strickland

Other books by Stephen H. Grant

Postales Salvadoreñas del Ayer/Early Salvadoran Postcards. San Salvador, El Salvador: Fundación María Escalón de Núñez, 1999, Bilingual edition.

Former Points of View: Postcards and Literary Passages from Pre-Independence Indonesia. Jakarta, Indonesia: Lontar, 1995.

Images de Guinée (with P. Durr, B. Sivan, E. Tompapa). Conakry, Guinea: Imprimerie Mission Catholique, 1st ed. 1991, 2nd ed. 1994.

Peter Strickland

New London Shipmaster
Boston Merchant
First Consul to Senegal

STEPHEN H. GRANT

An ADST-DACOR Diplomats and Diplomacy Book

NEW ACADEMIA PUBLISHING

New Academia Publishing
Washington, DC

First published by New Academia Publishing, 2007

The views and opinions in this book are solely those of the author and not necessarily those of the Association for Diplomatic Studies and Training or Diplomatic and Consular Officers, Retired.

Printed in the United States of America

Library of Congress Control Number: 2006936786
ISBN 978-0-9787713-3-1 paperback (alk. paper)

NAP
NEW ACADEMIA
PUBLISHING

New Academia Publishing, LLC
P.O. Box 27420 - Washington, DC 20038-7420
www.newacademia.com - info@newacademia.com

Contents

Illustrations and Chapter Display Sources   v

Foreword   xi

Acknowledgements   xiii

Preface   xv

1 Child of New London   1

2 Sailor on the Atlantic   11

3 Author from Boston   49

4 Merchant in West Africa   63

5 Resident on Gorée Island   83

6 Consul to Senegal   113

7 Retiree in Dorchester   145

8 Summary and Conclusions   167

Epilogue   175

Notes   177

Peter Strickland Genealogy   187

Peter Strickland Chronology   188

Bibliography   189

About the Author   192

Indices   193

   People   193

   Places   195

   Vessels   197

   General   200

Illustrations

1. Peter Strickland portrait.
   The National Cyclopaedia of American Biography (New York: James T. White Co., 1899), vol. 9, page 503. — Cover, 41

2. Strickland House, New London, Conn.
   Photo by James Finley. Used by permission. — 41

3. Strickland House, Boston, Mass.
   Photo by Christraud Geary. Used by permission. — 42

4. Strickland House, Gorée Island, Senegal.
   Photo by author. — 43

5. Envelope to Strickland from Boston, Mass., 1889.
   Author's collection. — 44, Back cover

6. Envelope to Strickland from Clarksville, Tenn., 1905. Author's collection. — 44

7. Strickland's first journal entry, Jan. 1, 1857.
   Peter Strickland Papers, University of Delaware Library, Newark, Del., folder 1. Used by permission. — 45

8. Printed full-rigged ship from cover page of "Journal of Voyages on the *Indian Queen, Robert Wing,* commanded by Peter Strickland," Oct. 28, 1864. © Mystic Seaport, Peter Strickland Manuscript Collection 69, G. W. Blunt White Library, Mystic, Conn., vol. 1. Used by permission. — 46

9. Marine note of protest, Apr. 8, 1886.
   Department of State, U.S. National Archives and Records Administration Record Group 84, US Consulate at Gorée-Dakar, 1883–1905, vol. 12. — 47

10. Strickland pencil drawing of a half brig, Jan. 14, 1866. © Mystic Seaport, Peter Strickland Manuscript Collection 69, G. W. Blunt White Library, Mystic, Conn., vol. 2. Used by permission.   Cover   104

11. Strickland pencil drawing of towed half brig, March 15, 1866. © Mystic Seaport, Peter Strickland Manuscript Collection 69, G. W. Blunt White Library, Mystic, Conn., vol. 2. Used by permission.   104

12. Log book Voyages of the *Zingarella* of Boston, Oct. 15, 1869. © Mystic Seaport, Peter Strickland Manuscript Collection 69, G. W. Blunt White Library, Mystic, Conn., vol. 3. Used by permission.   105

13. Title page to book by Peter Strickland, *A Voice from the Deep* (Boston: A. Williams & Company, 1873).   106

14. Postcard of U.S. consulate, with Strickland pencil drawing and labels, 1901. Department of State, U.S. National Archives and Records Administration Record Group 59, "Dispatches from U.S. Consul in Gorée-Dakar, French West Africa, 1883–1906."   107

15. Postcard showing welcome ceremony for British Governor of Bathurst Sir George Clinton on Gorée Island, Senegal, June 27, 1904. Author's collection.   108

16. Letter from Peter Strickland to French authorities about a shipwreck, 1895. National Archives, Dakar, Senegal. Folder 3 G 2/105 on consulates, 1885–1906.   109

17. Letter from Peter Strickland about Panama, 1904. National Archives, Dakar, Senegal. Folder 10 F 5 on US consulates, 1893–1921.   110

18. Peter Strickland gravestone, New London, Conn. Photo by author.   111

19. George Strickland gravestone, New London, Conn. Photo by author.   112

20. Presidents Abdou Diouf and Bill Clinton on Gorée Island, Senegal, April 2, 1998. Photo by Andrew Baird. Used by permission.   Back cover

21. Author and first U.S. consulate in Senegal. Photo by Djibril Albert Ndiaye.   Back cover

Chapter Display Sources

Preface

22. Printed drawing of a full-rigged ship from *Zingarella* log book, Oct. 15, 1869. © Mystic Seaport, Peter Strickland Manuscript Collection 69, G. W. Blunt White Library, Mystic, Conn., vol. 3. Used by permission.   xv

Chapter 1 – Child of New London

23. Strickland signature and address from *Indian Queen* journal of voyages, Oct. 28, 1864. © Mystic Seaport, Peter Strickland Manuscript Collection 69, G. W. Blunt White Library, Mystic, Conn., vol. 1. Used by permission.   1

Chapter 2 – Sailor on the Atlantic

24. Strickland signature as shipmaster, noting crew and cargo, Apr. 3, 1888. National Archives and Records Administration, Record Group 84, vol. 15:184.   11

Chapter 3 – Author from Boston

25. Strickland signature from *Zingarella* log book, Oct. 15, 1869. © Mystic Seaport, Peter Strickland Manuscript Collection 69, G. W. Blunt White Library, Mystic, Conn., vol. 3. Used by permission.   49

Chapter 4 – Merchant in West Africa

26. French business letter to Strickland, July 27, 1901. National Archives and Records Administration, Record Group 84, vol. 13.   63

Chapter 5 – Resident on Gorée Island
27. Department of State letter no. 168 to Strickland, Feb. 2, 1899. National Archives and Records Administration, Record Group 84, vol. 6.   83

Chapter 6 – Consul to Senegal
28. Peter Strickland consular dispatch to Department of State, Dec. 26, 1883. National Archives and Records Administration, Record Group 59.   113

Chapter 7 – Retiree in Dorchester
29. Peter Strickland consular dispatch to Department of State, Oct. 6, 1883. National Archives and Records Administration, Record Group 84.   145

Chapter 8 – Summary and Conclusions
30. Strickland pencil drawing of bark entitled "Homeward Bound," Jan. 29, 1866. © Mystic Seaport, Peter Strickland Manuscript Collection 69, G. W. Blunt White Library, Mystic, Conn., vol. 2. Used by permission.   167

Tables

Table 1. Complete List of Vessels Strickland Sailed in, 1852–1857   13

Table 2. Partial List of Vessels Strickland Sailed in, 1859–1905.   40

Table 3. Cargo from Boston to Gorée-Dakar on Board Bark *Jennie Cushman*, July 19, 1886.   74

Table 4. Cargo from Gorée-Dakar to Boston on Board Bark *Jennie Cushman*, Aug. 14, 1886.   75

Table 5. Class, Name, Home Port, and Owner of the Seventy-Eight Sailing Vessels from the United States Stopping at Gorée-Dakar in Senegal, West Africa, 1884–1904.   80-81

Table 6. Assets in Strickland Will.   164

Maps

Map 1. Captain Strickland's Routes to West Africa.   xxviii
Map 2. Captain Strickland's West Africa.   xxix

Foreword

The Association for Diplomatic Studies and Training (ADST) is an independent nonprofit organization dedicated to supporting the training of U.S. foreign affairs personnel and promoting knowledge of U.S. diplomacy. Among its activities in pursuit of the latter goal is the Diplomats and Diplomacy book series sponsored jointly with Diplomatic and Consular Officers, Retired, Inc. (DACOR). Created in 1995, the series is designed to increase public knowledge and appreciation of the involvement of American diplomats in world history. Stephen Grant's biography *Peter Strickland: New London Shipmaster, Boston Merchant, First Consul to Senegal* adds to our knowledge of what diplomats do and how they do it.

Most of us are familiar with the responsibilities today of American consular officials abroad. They screen visa applicants, issue visas and passports, record births, marriages, and deaths of Americans, and look after the welfare and whereabouts of their fellow citizens. Fewer know that over a century ago the predominant role of most U.S. consuls was to monitor and facilitate American shipping abroad and, in accordance with new legislation of the period, to look out for the welfare of American seamen.

In this book Grant tells us how a Connecticut Yankee, Peter Strickland, played that role as he attempted to survive and prosper in the midst of a strong French colonial presence in Senegal over the period 1864–1905. We learn that Strickland may have known more about West African trade than any other American at that time. Through 272 dispatches sent to the Department of State, he did his best to educate the American diplomatic and commercial establishment about the potential for trade with Africa.

Strickland carried out his consular duties in Senegal for over twenty years without a salary, renting his own office and lodgings and paying his own passage to reach his post and when returning to the United States on leave. Although allowed to practice an import-export business and keep the fees charged to American ships calling at Dakar, St. Louis, Rufisque, and Gorée, Strickland earned little else. He suffered from malaria and catarrh and nearly lost his daughter to yellow fever. Tragically, his son drowned off the coast of Dakar.

Because many have regarded the political side of diplomacy as the more prestigious career path, the contributions of our consuls have been too often ignored. Grant has taken a significant step toward remedying this misconception. To tell the story, he researched his subject for over five years, locating little-known Strickland documents in libraries in the eastern United States and unearthing Strickland's correspondence with French authorities in the Senegalese national archives.

Like Peter Strickland, Stephen Grant is a New Englander who spent most of his professional career in francophone West Africa, in Grant's case as a Foreign Service officer serving with USAID. And, like Strickland, he is an established author. As senior fellow at ADST, he assists retired diplomats in the preparation of their manuscripts for publication. We are pleased to add his own work of historical biography to our series.

KENNETH L. BROWN, *President*
Association for Diplomatic Studies and Training
www.adst.org

MICHAEL E. C. ELY, *President*
Diplomatic and Consular Officers, Retired
www.dacorbacon.org

Acknowledgements

The author would like to thank those who helped and encouraged him during the conception, research, writing, and editing stages and the occasional computer provocation:

Association for Diplomatic Studies and Training: Kenneth L. Brown, Margery Thompson, Marilyn Bentley, Kate Tussey.
Department of State, Office of the Historian: Paul Claussen, Evan Duncan.
United States National Archives and Records Administration: Milton Gustafson, Michael Hussey.
Senegal National Archives: Saliou Mbaye, Mamadou Ndiaye, Papa Momar Diop.
Institut Fondamental d'Afrique Noire, Senegal: Abdoulaye Camara, Père Joseph Roger de Benoist, Françoise and Cyr Descamps, Youssouph Mbargane Guissé.
Library of Congress: Marieta Harper, Mary Kramer.
Mystic Seaport, G. W. Blunt White Library: Paul O'Pecko, Leah Prescott, Wendy Schnur.
University of Delaware at Newark, Morris Library: Timothy D. Murray, Rebecca Johnson Melvin, Tammy Kiter, Shelly McCoy.
Dorchester Historical Society: James Cool, Earl Taylor.
New London County Historical Society: Pat Schaeffer.
Waterford Historical Society: Jerry Theiler.
Librarians: Norman Stevens, Martha MacPhail, Fatou Kinney Cissé, Charles Husbands, Laurie Deredita, Brian Rogers, Marcia Stewart, Beverly Erikson, Hugh Howard.
Gorée Friends: Moussa Diallo, Loulou Lapolice, Mass Tandine, Sylvain Sankalé, Marie-José Crespin, Xavier Ricou, Martin Schlumberger, Bruno Floury, Christian Lienhardt, Christian Saglio.
Friends: Lannon Walker, William Weary, Elizabeth and Lou Auld, Lisa and Jim Finley, Sarah Genton, Christraud Geary, Theodore

Mann, Ndiouga Adrien Benga, Sylvie Carduner, Paul Carduner, Olivier Carduner and Pat Ramsey, Charles Potin, Binta Angrand, Jane Loeffler, Dolores and Jim Strickland, Warren Schwartz, Sam Stokes, Gerry Stefon, Jesse Swingle, Maya Christy, Washington Biography Group members.

Preface

A purchase on eBay led to the writing of this book. In the 1990s, I had published three books in three continents: in Conakry, Guinea; in Jakarta, Indonesia; and in San Salvador, El Salvador. I based each book on vintage picture postcards I had collected as a hobby, tracing the social history of each country over the period 1900–1950. I wrote the books as a side interest while serving as manager of local education projects for the U.S. Agency for International Agency (USAID).

In the year 2000, I was assigned to USAID headquarters in Washington to be "desk officer" for several West African countries. In particular, I provided support from Washington for USAID programs in Senegal. Since other authors had already produced superb volumes[1] featuring evocative postcards of Senegal as a French colony, I resolved to identify a different topic somehow connected to Senegal for a new book. Seeking inspiration, I opened the online auction site eBay, registered as a new member, and typed in "Senegal" as my category of interest.

After a minute's wait a list of about one hundred items for sale appeared, including sets of old postage stamps, the national flag, old postcards, Senegal parrot T-shirts, and a hand-carved *djembe* drum. Then my gaze stopped on an envelope bearing a handsome blue three-cent stamp of President James Garfield—and beautifully penned in 1889 to a "Capt. Peter Strickland, U.S. Consul, Gorée, West Africa." I successfully bid on the item.

When the envelope arrived in the mail, I looked it over carefully. The skillfully opened envelope contained no letter or return address. Further examination revealed three faint postmarks on the back as well as two clear postmarks on the front side. The correspondent had written "via Bordeaux" on the address side. Using a magnifying glass to make out some of the cancellation marks, I was able to piece together the itinerary of the mysterious and enticing envelope. The letter had left Boston on August 2, 1889, and arrived in Paris on August 11. The back of the envelope was postmarked August 12 in Bordeaux and August 13 in Marseilles, suggesting that the letter was rerouted to catch a steamship leaving earlier from that port for Africa. After Bordeaux, Marseilles was the second most important trading port between France and its African possessions. The letter arrived on August 22 in Gorée, Senegal. Twenty days from Boston to Gorée in 1889; sometimes it takes as long today!

Eager to know more about my eBay treasure, I hastened to learn the identity of Capt. Peter Strickland. I e-mailed the Office of the Historian at the State Department to see if they had any records on Strickland, consul to West Africa. State Department historical files included only the barest information: Strickland came from Connecticut, received a recess appointment in 1883 to become the first consul in Senegal, and resigned from the consular service in 1906. The office admitted that it had no record of his postcareer activities. They did suggest, however, that I contact the National Archives and Records Administration (NARA), where his original consular dispatches should be housed.

At this point, I still had no clear notion as to what sort of book I would write, but with much excitement, I contacted NARA. Two 35mm microfilm reels contained the dispatches sent by Strickland to the State Department; I purchased copies by mail. The reels contain nearly 900 pages, centered on 272 dispatches from Senegal to Washington, D.C. Some of the consecutively numbered dispatches were accompanied by printed consular forms, which the consul had filled out. Strickland sent some dispatches and letters while on leave in the United States. In addition to the reports, the consul had sent maps, newspaper clippings, photos, and postcards. Not many diplomats send postcards to the State Department.

I pounced on a postcard Strickland had sent in 1905, labeled, "244. SENEGAL – Gorée – ensemble du port," showing the port area of Gorée in Senegal. Over a white building, Strickland had hand-drawn an oversized flagpole displaying a flag.[2] He labeled the building, "Position consular office." When I saw the consulate's location on the island, a conspicuous spot overlooking the wharf area, I wondered right away whether the building had survived.

Gorée Island is notorious because West Africans taken into bondage were packed onto slave ships there to make the long Atlantic crossing to the Americas. It is also known as a strategic military and economic outpost that frequently changed hands among colonial powers: Portuguese, Dutch, British, and French. Before Dakar, Gorée served as the capital of French West Africa.

As soon as I could manage a trip to Africa, I took the twenty-minute ferry ride from Dakar on the mainland to Gorée. Approaching the wharf, I spotted the imposing building, now painted crimson and ochre like many of the colorful Gorée houses. A tall, bearded Frenchman in shorts answered my knock at the door of the first American consulate in Senegal. I introduced myself, explaining my interest in the U.S. consul who had lived there. When, in the course of the conversation, he revealed that he was renting the house, I asked who the owner was. He replied, "A French doctor who lives in Paris." "What is his name?" I pursued. "Martin Schlumberger," came the answer. My jaw dropped. I exclaimed to him, *"Mais, Martin, c'est mon cousin."* He's my cousin.

I had last seen Martin, a distant cousin by marriage on my mother's side, thirty years before in Fada Ngourma in the West African country of Burkina Faso (then Upper Volta). I phoned him that evening from a *télé-centre* on Gorée and promised to see him in Paris on my way back to the United States. We had a lot of catching up to do.

In this research project, not only was I learning a lot about Strickland. I was finding out something about myself. My family had played a role in the Strickland story: it owned the building housing the first American consulate in French West Africa. In conducting historical research in Senegal, I had become part of the story.

Chance and coincidence thus marked the genesis of this book. But who did Capt. Peter Strickland turn out to be? Only two common references to Peter Strickland exist on library shelves. A century ago, the rank of consul qualified its holder for listing in a *Who's Who* publication. Strickland never made it into the national *Who's Who*, but he did appear in the first (1909) and second (1916) editions of the regional version, *Who's Who in New England*. Here is the earlier entry.

STRICKLAND, PETER, consul; *b.* Montville, Conn., Aug. 1, 1837; *s.* Peter R. and Laura (White) S.; ed. pub. schs., Montville and New London, and under tuition of father; *m.* New London, Conn., June 11, 1861, Mary Louise Rogers. Taught sch. in Conn. at 15; adopted sea faring life and was 2d mate of ship at 19, chief mate at 20, master at 24; engaged in African trade from Boston as capt. and later as capt. and supercargo, continuing until 1877 when became agt. in Africa; Am consul, French W. Africa, since 1883; lived in tropical Africa about 30 yrs. *Address,* 102 Neponset Av., Boston.[3]

Secondly, a well-known reference work on eighteenth- and nineteenth-century personalities: *The National Cyclopaedia of American Biography,* published in 1899,[4] devotes a column to Peter Strickland, illustrated with his engraved portrait.

Combining these sources, we meet a man with five occupations to his credit: schoolteacher, book author, shipmaster, merchant, and consul. When he was not aboard a ship, he divided his life between the New England seacoast (New London and Boston) and Senegal, West Africa (Dakar and Gorée Island). Strickland was also a family man: he married a New Londoner and fathered two boys and two girls.

A visit to the Cedar Grove Cemetery in New London revealed his family's fate, through records in the cemetery office and city hall and the 16 x 25 foot family burial plot. A nine-foot high granite stone displays dates and epitaphs on each of its four sides. The first to perish was the consul's firstborn and namesake: baby Peter Strickland died of bronchitis in New London in 1863 at age ten months. Next was the second son, George, who died in 1888 at age twenty-three by accidentally drowning off the coast of West Africa, where he was serving his father as vice consul. The second daughter, Grace, died in Boston of diphtheria in 1906, aged thirty-one. Only the first daughter, Mary, lived a long life, dying in Boston of bronchial pneumonia in 1945 at age seventy-seven. Their mother and Captain Strickland's wife, Mary Louise Rogers, lived to eighty-two, dying in Boston in 1915. No cause appeared in any known record. Peter Strickland himself died in Boston of arterial sclerosis in

1921 at age eighty-three. No child had married; the Peter Strickland line died out.

Library reference works, family gravestones, and consular dispatches provided skeletal information on the man who became the first American consul to Senegal and French West Africa. An internet search via Google revealed that two library repositories in the eastern United States housed important collections of Peter Strickland's papers: the Mystic Seaport Library in Mystic, Connecticut, and the University of Delaware Library in Newark.

These papers contain ship logs that Captain Strickland neatly kept; business ledgers that merchant Strickland maintained, with names of business partners, lists of expenditures, and inventories of ship cargoes; and "letter-books," hardbound albums filled with yellow carbon copies of letters Strickland wrote, mainly on business topics but including a few family letters. The carbon impression is often faint and hard to read. There are over 2,000 letters, the first written in 1876, and the last in 1921.

Finally, the papers include Strickland's personal journal, the most valuable source of all. His first entry was in 1857, when he set out as second mate on a sea voyage to Europe at the age of nineteen. His last entry was in the year of his death. In his later years, Strickland copied his early diaries—which had survived in his wooden seaman's chest—into hardbound albums. What this means is that the records are much more legible than they might have been; in many cases, they are still in mint condition. The journal covers a sixty-four-year span and contains over 2,500 pages.

When I had finally read through all the journal pages, however, I realized that the entries covered only twenty-five years—less than the sixty-four years the journal purported to cover and less than one half of Strickland's adult life. In addition, dozens of pages have clearly been ripped out. A bookmark I found in one letter-book offered a clue. It consisted of a clipping from the *Boston Transcript* dated Aug. 30, 1924, three years after the captain's death. Someone had been looking through his papers. Who? Daughter Mary? Perhaps she lived with the family memorabilia for another two decades.

I decided to write a biography, touching on all aspects of Strickland's long life, and relying heavily on his astonishing journal.

Attempting to fill the gaps in information available in the Strickland papers, I widened my search, using modern technology. Logging onto an online bulletin board devoted to Strickland genealogy, I posted a message announcing my research project on Captain Peter Strickland, telling all Stricklands that I was looking for Peter's photograph. A few weeks later, I received a reply on the bulletin board: "I do not have a photograph of Peter Strickland for you, but I think I live in his house."

I began an exchange of e-mails with this correspondent, who had recently purchased a farmhouse that belonged to a Peter Strickland in the mid-1700s. A 1754 deed found in the New London land records indicates that Peter Strickland purchased eighty acres of land on the Norwich Road from the Rogers brothers. I discovered there were actually eight Peter Stricklands from the mid-1600s to the 1900s. The New London farmhouse, built on a large tract of land, belonged to the great grandfather of "our" Peter Strickland. He passed it down to his son and grandson (Peter's father), who sold it in 1833, four years before Peter was born. Nevertheless, it was an imposing house on the Norwich Road that Peter may have known as a youth. As a young boy, Peter Strickland may also have known that on September 6, 1781, when Benedict Arnold burned New London during the Revolutionary War, the townspeople fled the coastal areas. They sought refuge in farmhouses along the Norwich Road, perhaps finding shelter at the home of great grandfather Peter Strickland (1718–1801).

I learned that a Strickland couple in California had compiled a genealogy of the "Descendants of Peter Strickland." I obtained a copy. It covers the period 1646–1907. Another Strickland living in Connecticut put together genealogical "pedigrees" of the Peter Strickland family with seals and arms. The last few years have witnessed the development of a "Strickland DNA Project Website," where one can follow the attempts to track and match family members across the United States. The family gets together for summer reunions.

In New London, I spent hours looking through documents in the Rare Books Room at the Public Library. While many volumes gave me information on the city's history, I found very few references to any Peter Strickland.

In the New London city hall, I went through several of the annual New London city directories. In the 1863 issue, I found P. Strickland listed as a mariner living at 15 Blinman St. Strickland had given this address in his journal. His neighbor at 13 Blinman St. was his older brother, Henry Rogers Strickland. The two Strickland brothers married two Rogers sisters. The Rogers family owned both houses. Street names and numbers have changed in this neighborhood, however, and the neighborhood has been renovated.

In the Norwich city hall, New London county census records from July 1860 note that the value of the personal estate of Peter Strickland, seaman, age twenty-three, was $500. The same census sheet includes an item on his father, Peter Rogers Strickland: farmer, age fifty-five, value of real estate $2,500, value of personal estate $2,700; and an item on his mother, stating that Laura Strickland, housekeeper, was age fifty-one. In the younger Peter Strickland, we have the son of moderately well off parents who leaves the family farm.

I visited the town hall in Montville, Connecticut, where Peter Strickland was born. I found nothing on my Peter Strickland, but by reading through local school committee minutes, I did discover that his father was a member of the Montville school committee in 1851 and 1859. That is important, for it reveals something about the Stricklands' values. I would recall this family interest in education when I later read letters Peter Strickland wrote to his son in the 1870s on the importance of a good education.

Continuing my pursuit of Strickland material in Massachusetts, I traveled to the Peabody Essex Institute in Salem. Its Phillips Library had a copy of Peter Strickland's book, *A Voice from the Deep*,[5] in its original gilt-stamped binding, but nothing else on him. However, I found the records of sea captains out of Salem in the 1840s and 1850s on their trading in West Africa. These records provided helpful context for Strickland's later experiences in West Africa. Sea captains from Salem frequented mainly British colonies, while Strickland concentrated on the French colony of Senegal and, to some extent, on the Portuguese colony of Bissau (now Guinea Bissau).

Another mystery in following the Strickland story is that no identifiable family possessions appear to have survived. In his journal entries, the consul relates how he had his houseboy pack up crate upon crate of artifacts from Africa. In particular, he mentioned six ostrich eggs and a stuffed crocodile, bracelets and mounted lions' teeth, and lion and leopard skins. He also refers to three-quarters of a ton of books from his personal library shipped back to Boston. Where are these personal belongings?

From Suffolk County in Boston, I purchased copies of Peter Strickland's will and that of his daughter Mary. The beneficiaries listed in the latter will are New London families. I have attempted to contact their descendants. While Strickland kept his personal possessions in Boston, he remained emotionally attached to his New London roots.

I visited the family house on Neponset Avenue in Dorchester, Massachusetts, wondering whether some might not still be stashed away in the attic. The front and back doors were locked, the garden overgrown. The mail carrier divulged that a Catholic nun had lived in the house but had died, and that the house had remained unoccupied for many months.

I inquired of the Delaware and Mystic libraries how they came to acquire the Strickland papers. Delaware bought the Strickland materials from Boston's Edward Morrill & Son, Rare and Scholarly Books & Prints in 1956. Mystic purchased its collection in 1966 from Goodspeed's Books of Boston. It is common for collections to be split up in this fashion. Could there be another lot of Strickland materials somewhere, unaccounted for?

Strickland's correspondence during retirement years mentions family photos his daughter Mary took, which were sent to Mr. Claude Potin, a close friend and neighbor on the Island of Gorée. When I visited Senegal, I arranged a meeting in Dakar with six Potin grandchildren, who admitted that they had nothing from their grandfather's possessions with the exception of one portrait of him. Alas, I was following a Strickland trail that was a century old.

At the time that Peter Strickland lived on Gorée Island, serving as consul as well as merchant, Senegal was a French colony. Strickland wrote many letters to the French authorities, as well as to French business associates and personal friends. Strickland's written French was atrocious. He had received no training in the French language in the United States before his posting to Senegal and apparently did little, outside of some everyday practice, to improve his written French while living abroad.

When Senegal became independent in 1960, the departing French colonial authorities left many archives behind. In Dakar, to my great pleasure, I came across a few original letters Strickland handwrote on U.S. consular stationery. Two are reproduced in this book.

During several visits to the National Archives and Records Administration (NARA) in College Park, Maryland, I discovered a major treasure trove: besides microfilmed nine hundred pages of Strickland dispatches, I came upon sixteen volumes comprising 1,850 pages of consular records, many written in Strickland's hand. One volume gives the complete list of fees the consulate charged during more than twenty years. Others include return messages from the State Department to Strickland, department instructions to the consul, invoices, and a list of all American vessels docking in Senegal. In an album on the Sierra Leone shelf, I even located a mis-filed envelope with an original letter written by Strickland in 1901. The letter, on Gorée-Dakar consulate stationery, was addressed to a ship captain whose vessel was grounded off the coast.

A challenge in writing this biography is that, although we know what Peter Strickland thought of many events and people during his journey through life, we are unable to balance his views with the perceptions of those who knew him. I had hoped to find a copy of the eulogy read by Reverend J. Beveridge Lee, D.D., in 1921 at his gravesite by visiting the Second Congregational Church in New London. However, the church said its records do not contain eulogies going back to the 1920s. There has not been a family repository for his papers since his daughter died in 1945.

Three short quotations assert claims to fame for Strickland's long, well-documented, and remarkable life. In 1881, he wrote from Senegal to a business associate in Boston, "There is probably at the present time no living American who knows as much about this Coast trade as myself."[6] Trade historians will find in Strickland's journal and correspondence much detailed description of African commerce.

In 1898, Strickland wrote in his journal, "I have crossed the Atlantic more than a hundred times in charge of a vessel."[7] Maritime historians could add Strickland's name to a list of other captains who could boast as much.

In the same year, he wrote to a friend, "Your humble servant is the only American that I know of between the Straits of Gibraltar and Sierra Leone."[8] Strickland was one lonely American toiling in an expanse of territory 1,500 miles long.

The chapters in this book follow Strickland's life chronologically, from "Child of New London" to "Retiree in Dorchester." In between are four chapters that focus on his sea voyages and African stays. Because Strickland pursued more than one career at a time, some overlap occurs during this chronological progression. Some readers may find the level of detail in the Gorée chapter generous, but I have tried to compensate for the dearth of available written accounts of life on this island. As a retiree, Strickland had more time to devote to his journal. A final chapter sums up the Strickland story and highlights his contributions. To give readers a sense of Captain Strickland's routes from the United States to Africa and back and an understanding of the West African territories where he traded, two maps are included in the next section.

Reading Strickland's elegant handwritten journal, dispatches, and letters is a pleasure for the eyes. One loves to follow the flourishes with which he ornamented the "D" of Dakar, the "G" of Gorée, and the "H" of Honorable.

Some of Strickland's expressions are amusingly pithy. As a young sailor, he met American consuls "never burdened with honesty." On Gorée Island during the rainy season, his income from American ships paying port fees amounted to a "beggarly pittance." In Dorchester, he bought a vacuum cleaner from an "oily-tongued agent." In retirement, he "spent the day existing."

The more I read and enjoyed Strickland's writing, the more I felt that his biography should feature his prose. The reader will therefore find liberal selections of quoted material. Strickland's style is typical of his era for its lack of punctuation, variant spellings, and frequent capitalization of important words in mid-sentence. I have retained his original usages. For a lad who left school at age fifteen, he developed an engagingly expressive style.

Concerned that he had written his early journals on cheap paper and in leaky ships, Strickland in 1913 and 1914 devoted months of his retirement to recopying them. In one album, the year marked at the top of each page suddenly switches from 1857 to 1914. Inadvertently, he had written the year in which he was recopying rather than the year of the initial entry.

Did Strickland take advantage of his rewrite to alter his earlier versions of events? He claims that his major change was rectifying dates. It took him up to a month to redo one year's worth of entries, a major activity for a seventy-seven-year-old. He admits to delight in reliving early episodes in his life. He is especially glad to achieve uniformity in the size and appearance of his new journal albums, 8 x 11 inch hard-backed volumes purchased at a stationer's in Boston. Each album generally contains two hundred or four hundred prenumbered pages, making it easy to track and find the dated entries. How nice it would be if this first biography of Peter Strickland led to the discovery of some of his missing journal albums.

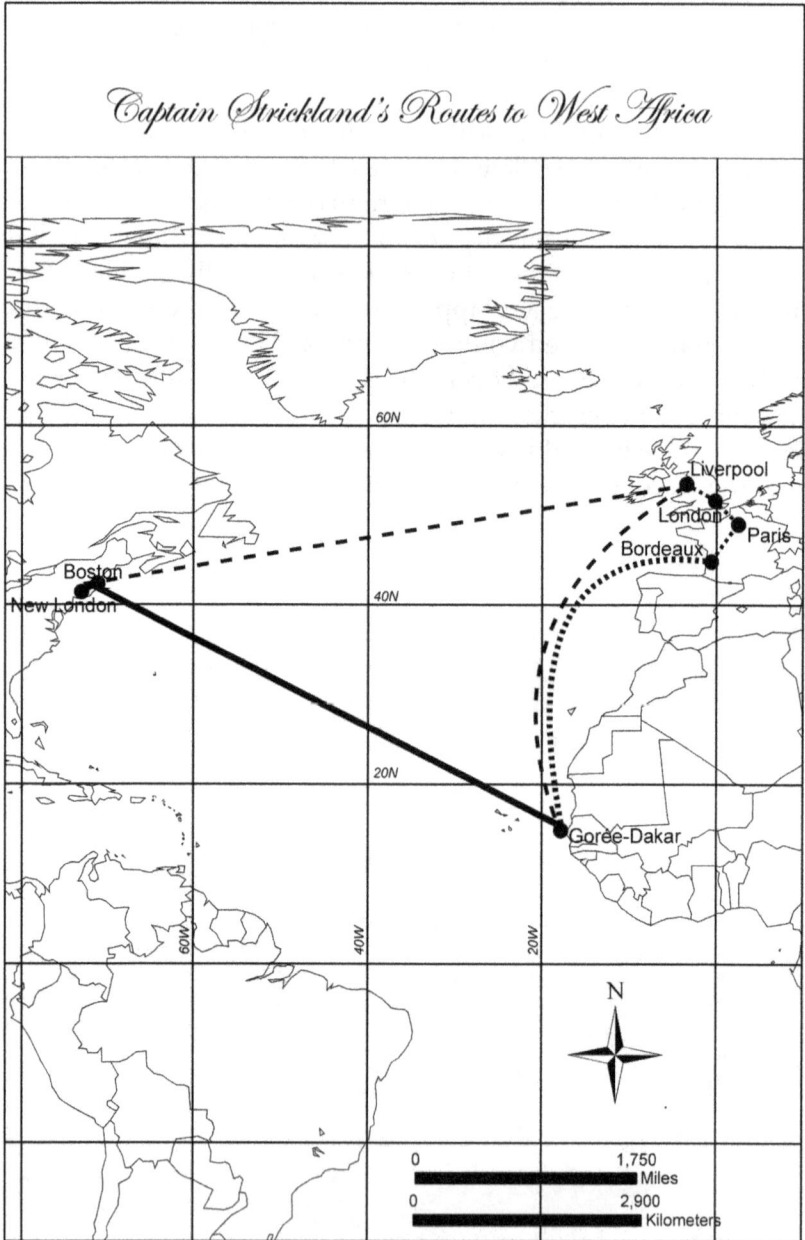

Captain Strickland's Routes to West Africa

Liverpool
London
Paris
Bordeaux
Boston
New London
40N
60N
20N
60W
40W
20W
Gorée-Dakar

N

| 0 | 1,750 |
Miles
| 0 | 2,900 |
Kilometers

Created by Shelly McCoy, University of Delaware Library, ESRI Data and Maps, 2005

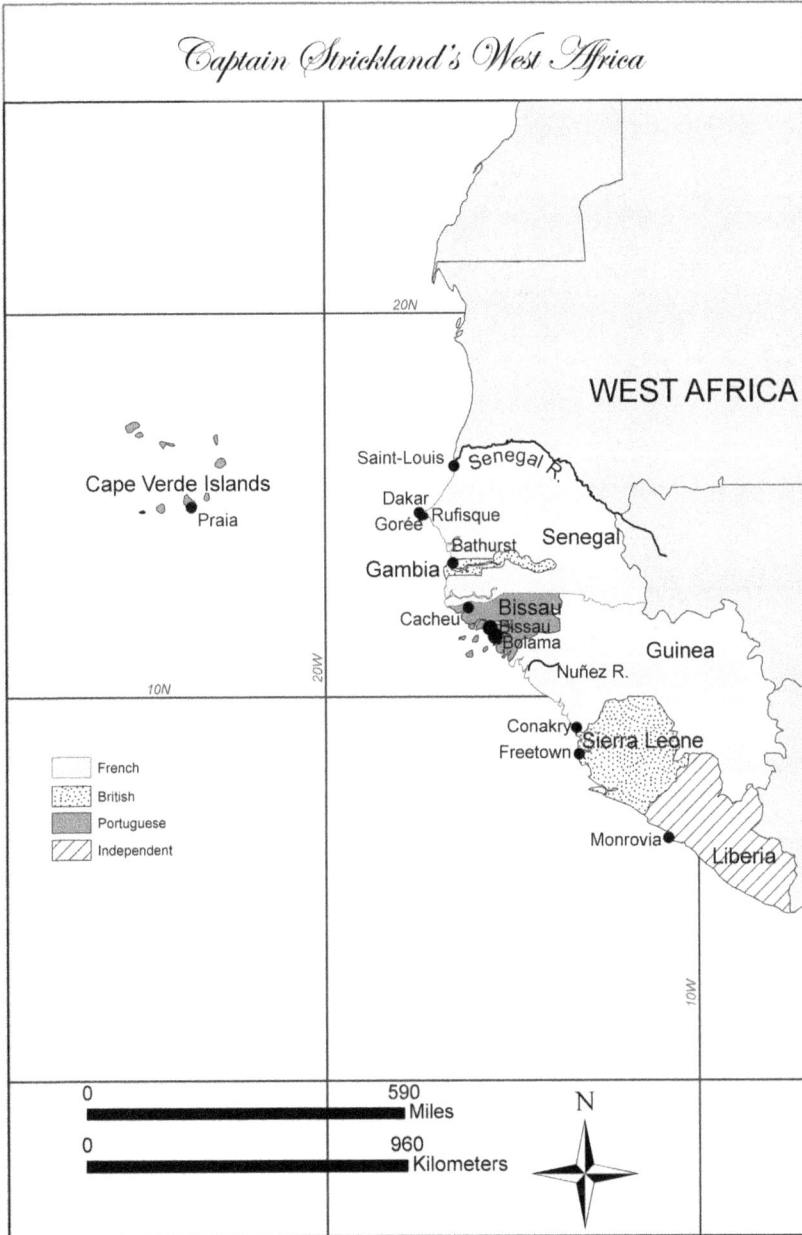

Captain Strickland's West Africa

WEST AFRICA

Cape Verde Islands
Praia

20N

Saint-Louis
Dakar
Gorée
Rufisque
Bathurst
Gambia
Cacheu
Bissau
Bissau
Bolama
Nuñez R.
Conakry
Freetown
Monrovia

Senegal R.
Senegal
Guinea
Sierra Leone
Liberia

10N
20W
10W

French
British
Portuguese
Independent

| 0 | 590 |
| Miles |
| 0 | 960 |
| Kilometers |

N

Created by Shelly McCoy, University of Delaware Library, ESRI Data and Maps, 2005

1

Child of New London

Peter Strickland
New London
Connecticut
U. S. A.

Peter Strickland was born in 1837, the third child of Peter Rogers Strickland and Laura White, in Montville, eight miles north of New London, Connecticut. We are fortunate to have over 7,000 archival pages on Peter Strickland the adult, but we know very little about his ancestry and early life. Frances Manwaring Caulkins states that a Peter Strickland (c1646–c1722) was among the first settlers of New London in the 1670s.[1] Ipswich court records in Massachusetts refer to a Peeter [sic] Strickland in 1669[2]: It is widely held that many original Massachusetts settlers migrated to Connecticut. As for ancestral origins across the Atlantic, the Strickland DNA Project referred to in the preface has recently cited Sizergh Castle in Cumbria County in northwestern England as a Strickland family home since the year 1239. This state-of-the-art genealogical quest through DNA is so far inconclusive.

This first Peter Strickland married Elizabeth Comstock of New London in 1673, and died in New London. The Stricklands and the Comstocks are among the oldest New London families of European origin. The family relationship involved real estate as well as marriage partners. In 1833, Peter Rogers Strickland (Capt. Peter Strickland's father) sold his house, built in about 1760, to Asa Comstock.

Between 1833 and 1867, Peter Rogers Strickland bought and sold many lots of land with farm buildings in Montville and in East Lyme. Peter's father was a farmer, one who had enough extra cash to indulge in land acquisitions. Yet he did not keep the land for long periods. In 1833, Strickland purchased fifty acres on the northerly side of Old Colchester Road in Montville, adjacent to land owned by the heirs of Zebediah Comstock. In 1844, he sold this property and purchased a tract containing 117 acres, on Fire St. in Montville, to the northwest of the previous property. This land included the second house that young Peter would have lived in.

In 1849, Strickland père sold the second property to another Asa Comstock and purchased farmland and a dwelling house on 175 acres, partly in the Chesterfield section of Montville and partly in East Lyme. This property is still standing; then the address was Walnut Hill Rd. and now it is Holmes Rd. He kept this third property until 1867, when Capt. Strickland would have been thirty years old and already involved in the African trade.

Besides the Comstocks, another old New London family closely allied with the Stricklands were the Rogers. James Rogers came to New London in 1660. His son John founded a controversial Protestant sect called the "Rogerenes." Dissenting from the predominant Congregational Church, Rogerenes believed in the equality of men and women, the abolition of slavery, respect for Native Americans, and temperance.[3] While Stricklands and Rogers intermarried for decades, no mention is made of Rogerenes in the Peter Strickland papers.

Peter Strickland had one older sister, Mary Ann, who died before he was born, one older brother, Henry Rogers, and one younger brother, Samuel White. Peter was closest to Henry. In their youth, they spent a lot of time together, taking long walks or going fishing. Henry built a fishing craft and Peter fitted it with mast and sail. They knew all the best places to find clams and crabs, their mother's favorite foods.

All three Strickland brothers began their professional lives as classroom teachers. This fact speaks very highly of their home education from a farmer father. When Henry was fifteen in 1845, he taught a class in mathematics to over fifty pupils. When Peter was fifteen in 1852, he taught a winter session.[4] This was the same year that Peter ceased being a student. In the early 1860s, Samuel became a teacher at the Jordan Village School in Waterford, Connecticut. Built in 1858 as the first brick two-story building in town, the school served boys and girls from four to sixteen years old. Today the town hall stands on the site of the school.

In 1846, Henry Strickland made a two-year voyage on the whaling bark *Exchange,* sailing out of New Bedford, Massachusetts.[5] The vessel stopped at the Cape Verde Islands off Senegal. Surely, Henry described his West African visit to Peter, who would eventually spend a third of his life in this region of the world. Henry then joined an early group of forty-niners who traveled to California around Cape Horn. Chosen colonel of a regiment, he was wounded by Indians. Subsequently, Henry left California for a brief period in the merchant marine. He called at ports in the West Indies, South America, and China. Peter undoubtedly heard about his older brother's adventurous life, but seldom refers to it in his journal. In 1852, the year Henry returned to Connecticut to settle down, Peter took to the sea.

Henry later married Martha Washington Rogers of the Rogers family mentioned above. When Henry and Martha's first son Charles was born, they sent Peter—on a merchant voyage in New Orleans—a lock of the baby's hair, which pleased the younger brother immensely.

Henry worked in business, including real estate, in Willimantic and in New London for a while until poor health forced him to retire. Returning to Montville where he had grown up, Henry served his town as a state legislator in 1879–1880, selectman, judge, and school principal. Around 1894, Henry and Martha moved to Terrell, Texas for his health. By this time, the two brothers had grown apart.

At age twenty, brother Samuel would marry Happy Lavinia Fanning. They lived in a farmhouse in Chesterfield on his parents' property, where he farmed the land and practiced civil engineering. Peter recorded his joy at finding Samuel's letters among his mail in foreign ports.

Peter was born in a farmhouse in Montville on land that he later claimed had become the property of Connecticut College. The college could not confirm this. In any case, it was nearby. Peter looked forward to the first Monday of November each year when school began. He first attended an old round schoolhouse (referred to in school committee notes in Montville town hall), which was demolished before 1860.[6] He attended school until age fifteen, the usual age for having completed public school. As his self-written *Who's Who* description states, Peter owed much of his education to his father. Peter would later pass down educational precepts to his own children, exhorting them via correspondence to study well and learn all they could. From Bissau in West Africa, he wrote his twelve-year-old son, "[w]hen I was of your age I learned all I could about farming."[7]

Upon retirement from the consular service in 1905, Strickland became a gentleman farmer in Dorchester, Massachusetts, but returned occasionally to New London. During these nostalgic visits, he often entered reminiscences into his journal concerning his youth. Invariably, the visits prompt him to compare the New London countryside of the 1840s with that of the early 1900s.

> Hired a carriage at the Livery stable on the corner of Brainerd and Amity Sts and drove up into the country on the "Old Colchester Road," the first road I was ever acquainted with and which has changed but little since I first passed over it. We passed on it the house where I was born and continued on as far as Schofields factory where we took lunch and watered our horse. Returning we soon came to the house of Miss Adeline Fellows, an old schoolmate of mine, whom I had not seen for 58 years. She never married, and has always lived at home in her fathers [sic] house, which has not changed in appearance in 60 years. . . . Soon after we left the Fellows Mansion we took a cross-road which led by a house on Dolbeare Hill where I lived with my parents for about five years between the ages of seven and twelve. I passed the same place with my cousin, Mr. Nathan Comstock, last August, but it was then crowded with Jews from New York, whereas now it seems like a lone hamlet in the midst of the woods. . . . We returned to New-London via Chapel-Hill, Chesterfield, Lakes Pond, and Cohansic. Near the last mentioned place we entered on a new and beautiful drive-way, a part of the Vauxhall Road, and saw on the left a couple of beautiful artificial Lakes which have not existed long. I was on the whole very much entertained by this trip, and Sika [Strickland's nickname for his daughter Mary] would have been only for the fright she had on account of the deep ruts of the cross-road and the fear that passing automobiles might scare our horse.[8]

One can imagine the seventy-year-old Peter Strickland at the reins of his carriage, enthusiastically pointing out to his daughter, thirty-nine-year-old Mary, all the familiar physical landmarks from his childhood. Aside from the presence of vacationing Jewish families from New York and the appearance of artificial lakes, Strickland easily recognized all that he encountered, even an acquaintance who had lived in the same house for almost sixty years. The skittish horse sharing the roadway with a noisy early automobile dramatizes the meeting of old and new.

Five years later, in 1912, Strickland caught a train back to New London with his daughter, and again they went on a nostalgic carriage ride.

Sika and I about eleven o'clock got a two-seated carriage from Buffums Livery stable and started for the house where I was born in Montville, intending to photograph it. In going there we passed along what used to be called the "Old Colchester Road" where I saw many objects which have not changed much in appearance during the last three quarters of a century. To a very large extent however things have changed even there, for most of the old houses which still exist although many of them have been remodeled while undergoing reparations, are inhabited by Russian Jews instead of the descendants of Anglo-Saxon stock, whose business in the main does not seem to be farming but keeping boarding-houses for their Jewish friends and relatives in New-York whose women & children come to them in great numbers to spend the summer months.

When we got to the house where I was born we found a girl only at home named Bertha Silverzweig whose father Benjamin Silverzweig with her brothers were away somewhere, it being the Jewish Sabbath. We found the girl to be bright and intelligent but not well satisfied with her lot as a farmers [sic] daughter. She longed she said to get away and travel. I think she is about twenty years of age and quite good looking. She did not ask us to enter the house which I could quite understand as I presume it was not in a state to be seen by visitors but she gave us a dozen peaches which were grown on the place, drew water from the house, and would accept nothing in payment, not even a gratuity.[9]

The 1917 New London directory lists Benjamin Silverzweig as a grocer. Strickland was discovering that the Montville area had become a popular place for families to rent places for the summer, near the Long Island Sound yet remote and quiet. Although Mary had intended to take a picture of her father's birthplace, she told her father she did not have the right photographic equipment and feared her snapshot would not come out. Mary was an avid photographer, taking pictures of her family and her homes in New London and in Boston, as well as in Senegal, where she even had a darkroom. Unfortunately, none of her photos is known to have survived.

Over time, Strickland's family had moved from agricultural lands closer to the seashore. At age fifteen, Peter left New London for a seafarer's life. He was not alone, as other extended family members had been sailors and he had relatives lost at sea. When Peter came back between voyages, he would visit his parents on Walnut Hill in Chesterfield or the Comstock in-laws in Uncasville, both small towns north of New London.

While it may have required a good measure of independence and resolve for Peter to abandon the farming life of his ancestors, life at sea was a familiar alternative. His older brother had showed him the way. Earlier many New Londoners had participated in Revolutionary War privateering. Second only to New Bedford, Mass., New London, with its superb natural harbor, was the busiest whaling port in New England, as well as a major center for coastal and world trade.

Peter had opportunities to enter other lines of work. Brother-in-law Orlando Rogers offered him a steady carpenter's job for $26 a month. Brother Henry tried to lure him into a partnership to manage a dairy farm. Instead, he studied Nathaniel Bowditch's *American Practical Navigator*, along with bookkeeping and physiology texts, to improve his chances of advancement in the merchant marine.

Throughout his youth and young adulthood, Peter Strickland was a regular churchgoer and frequent Bible reader. As a boy, he attended church in Palmerstown, a section of Montville. He first joined the church in Chesterfield. As a young adult, he joined the First Baptist Church of New London. His wife joined the same church, and was baptized by immersion near the New London customhouse on a very cold Sunday, January 4, 1863.

Strickland paid great attention to the sermons he heard, and often entered his opinion of them into his journal. He looked forward to returning to hear his favorite pastors. On one Sunday in 1859, he attended three services: in the morning at the First Congregational Church in New London, in the afternoon to hear a Quaker Methodist, and in the evening a revival meeting.[10] His brother's wife, Martha Rogers, had been encouraging him to attend revivalist services.

Religion was a major topic of conversation when the family met. He railed against sermons "permeated with Calvinism." He dismissed Christian Science as "harmless humbug." He considered that Unitarianism did not flourish because "the vast majority of people are not willing to believe Christ was only a man like themselves."[11] At various times in his life, he would go to prayer meetings every evening. He would also attend special chapel services for mariners.

Peter set forth from home for the sea with firm religious convictions and a strong sense of family values. He believed that Providence would follow him along the path of life. He vowed to be true to himself and be fair to others. He committed himself to lifelong learning.

As a young man aged twenty-four at the outbreak of the Civil War, Peter might have been drafted for military service. However, at age sixteen, he had lost the end of the index finger on his right hand due to an infection. On August 7, 1862, when Peter heard of the impending draft, he "went to see the examining physician Dr. Porter who as soon as he saw my right hand minus the fore-finger directed that I should have a certificate of exemption from military service and I was accordingly furnished with one."[12] The Union forces would not take a draftee lacking a trigger finger.

During the Civil War, Strickland pondered in his journal what his life might have been had he been inducted into the navy.

I spent the day in looking around for employment and in writing letters. If it had not been for the loss of the fore-finger of my right hand when I was about sixteen by a felon[13]

I should probably now be in the navy and not have to look up a chance for going to sea under difficult circumstances. If my station however were on board of a River Craft Gunboat where I could be tormented by mosquitoes on one of our Western Rivers I might be wishing myself here. Where one finds himself in a position esteemed by many to be disagreeable there are generally compensations.[14]

His rejection for service in a Connecticut unit did not mean that Strickland was completely shielded from the war. In 1864, he was with his family when the body of his cousin Tommy Rogers was brought to Chesterfield from Alexandria, Virginia, where he had died of a fever. Peter helped unload the coffin. His aunt and cousins then burst into "one heart-rending piercing wail which lasted half an hour. They ran from room to room and tore their hair in their grief which was simply dreadful to witness."[15] This was Peter Strickland's closest experience of the tragedy of war and he never forgot it.

2

Sailor on the Atlantic

J. Strickland, Master.

We know little about Strickland's early sea voyages, except for the names of the vessels he sailed in from 1852 to 1857. He gave the list in consecutive order:[1]

Table 1. Complete List of Vessels
Strickland Sailed in, 1852–1857

Schooner	*Clotilda*
Sloop	*Falcon*
Schooner	*Perseverance*
Brig	*Caroline*
Schooner	*Compliance*
Ship	*New Hampshire*
Schooner	*Colonel Satterly*
Schooner	*William A. Ellis*
Brig	*Dido*
Bark	*Charles William*
Bark	*Laconia*
Brig	*Galena*
Schooner	*Magdala*
Ship	*Ladoga*
Ship	*Lorenzo*
Ship	*Tranquebar*
Ship	*Oriental*
Bark	*Rhone*
Ship	*Seth Sprague*
Ship	*Mariner*
Bark	*Horace*
Schooner	*Inlian*
Ship	*Oxnard*
Brig	*New World*
Brig	*New York*
Brig	*F. C. Clark*
Bark	*Mary E. Dunworth*

These schooners, sloops, brigs, barks, and ships plied the Atlantic as part of the "coasting trade" between New London and points north and south. They were one-, two-, or three-masted vessels fifty to eighty feet long, with seventeen to twenty-five-foot beam and five to six-foot draft, weighing thirty-five to one-hundred tons. Most had been built in Connecticut or New York shipyards, and were often over twenty years old when young Peter walked aboard.

Going to sea at age fifteen in 1852, Peter began his merchant career as a cabin boy. Wages for common sailors in the 1850s in New London were $20 a month. March 2, 1857, was a big day for Peter Strickland when he first served as officer.

> This morning I was offered by Captain Baker the position of Second Mate of the *Mary E. Dunworth* at $25 per month, the usual wages for vessels of this class, which I immediately accepted and took my things aft. It seemed rather strange to me to leave my comrades of six months with whom I was on excellent terms and assume an attitude toward them different from what I had been in the habit of doing, but I knew that they would be reasonable and that I was used to the vessel, circumstances much in my favor in gaining experience to be an officer, and I realized, fully I think, that now there was an opportunity offered me I should be a fool of the greatest size not to accept it. Thus at the age of twenty years I commenced my career as an officer of a vessel engaged in the foreign trade, fully conscious that if I could maintain my position with some credit for the next few months I should have confidence enough in myself to stand for an Officer's berth thereafter and never have to content myself with being as I had been, just a common sailor.[2]

In January of 1860, Capt. Benjamin Watlington offered Strickland a berth as chief mate on the *Richard Alsop* bound for Liverpool. He would have additional duties, such as keeping the logbook and taking care of the cargo. His wages would increase to $45 a month. Strickland was particularly elated, as he did not have to spend even one night in a boarding house for sailors, which he found exceedingly expensive. The vessel would be loaded with cotton in New Orleans.

On December 1, 1863, the American consul in Nassau formally installed Peter Strickland as the master of the *Benjamin Willis* of Boston. The following Sunday, he organized a worship service on board the vessel.[3] This act, uncommon for an American sea captain, billowed naturally from the strong religious upbringing Strickland received from his family in New London. He believed that regular organized worship on shipboard could offer sailors words of inspiration and much needed models of behavior. As captain, he was now fully in charge at only twenty-three years old. As his vessel headed north, Strickland now looked at the coastline in a different way: this was enemy territory for him. His country was at war with itself and he was a northerner passing through southern territorial waters. He was glad to make it to Boston in ten days.

Exactly twenty years later, in the month of December 1883, Strickland would become an American consul himself. This diplomatic post, conferred by the federal government in Washington, D.C., was something the young New England sailor could by no means have predicted in Nassau. For the moment, he was wholly absorbed in bringing his cargo from one port to another, and outrunning any potential southern privateers looking to intercept vessels and goods.

Strickland divulged his salaries as an officer during his merchant marine career in a letter written in 1902 to the U.S. vice-consul in Madrid: "I first came into this business in the capacity of chief mate of a brig engaged in the trade at $45.00 per month. Later I was master of a small vessel at $60.00 a month, and then of a larger one at $85.00 per month, and finally of the largest one in the trade, a Bark called *Zingarella* for sailing which I had $90.00 per month."[4] A captain earned twice what a starting officer would earn, but still not enough to become comfortably well off. Strickland was persuaded that one reason why American sailors did not marry was that their wages were so low, not sufficient to support a family. Not marrying signified a bachelor life, often tending toward dereliction.

Peter Strickland chronicled his mariner life including many aspects relating to officers and crew. He describes different characteristics of the captains he served and what he thought of his commanding officer. He recounts incidents of sailor dissipation, from the viewpoint of a fellow common seaman, and then as an officer who has to deal with such behavior. Strickland's constant observations of sailor behavior as well as his own struggle to earn a living as a seafarer led him to write the only book he authored, *A Voice from the Deep,* on behalf of seamen. The next chapter will examine the issues raised in the volume. Strickland felt deeply for sailors, suffered with them, and strived to raise their standards. The first incident he depicts in detail is a humorous one, revealing both about sailors' lax behavior and the manner in which a captain decides to deal with it.

This day things occurred which afforded considerable amusement for some of the ships company at the expense of the Second Mate, a young Englishman named Wilby. In the generally pleasant weather which accompanied the trade winds, the Captain, who was accompanied by his wife who was a very nice lady, had seldom appeared on deck at night, but this morning a little before daylight, wishing to ascertain how his watch was being kept, he came softly up the after-companion way and looked around for the Officer on watch. Not seeing him where he should have been, he stept to the binnacle where I was steering to see if the ship was on her course, and finding everything right in that respect he mounted the steps which led to the promenade deck where he found the second mate stretched out on a settee and fast asleep. From thence without giving any alarm he proceeded to the main-deck where he found the man who should have been on the lookout, awake indeed, but in the forecastle reading a novel. He did [not] trouble this man any more than he had done so to the Second Mate, but on his return aft he let go the main topsail halliards which allowed the yard and sail to come down with such a fearful clatter that the noise waked everyone on board, and frightened the Second Mate who of course felt delinquent in his being suddenly awakened almost out of his wits. After giving the Second Mate a good scolding the Captain told him to go forward with the men of his watch and set the studdingsails, not that they would do much good for there was scarcely any wind, but to get the second mate and the men who composed his watch wide awake. The Captain further ordered the Second Mate to have the decks thoroughly washed when the day broke and then retired, no doubt amused himself, to his bed.[5]

Compared with some of the later references to officer and crew behavior, this episode of innocent fun appears light-hearted. The second mate's being non-American—in this case British—was not at all rare on American sailing vessels crossing the Atlantic. On this voyage, the crew was six: four Americans, a Dane, and an Irishman. Most are under twenty years old and none over twenty-five. None is married. Strickland later notes that most of the crews he sails with are composed of Americans, Irish, Canadians, Germans, and Danes.

From 1875 on, Strickland devotes himself exclusively to the African trade. He notes that there are relatively few African crewmembers on board sailing vessels between West Africa and America. He sees no reason why Africans could not do the job. In 1876, he makes a breakthrough in one case. "Got the *Zingarella*'s papers all ready for her to sail to high water in the afternoon when the captain reported 3 of his men sick. Capt McDonald and I went right to replace them with black men and succeeded."[6] Many of the West Africans that work in and around boats even today are from one particular ethnic group, the *Kru*. They are also referred to as *Krou*, *Kroumen*, or *Kroomen*. Originated from the Gold Coast (later renamed Ghana) and Ivory Coast, the Kru had a reputation for agility and industriousness.

The Strickland journal contains a "Kru story" worth recounting. It took place during the Civil War in New York. The tale demonstrates that even the American Civil War affected some West Africans.

Started for Boston on an early train but did not arrive there until about one P.M. I found on my arrival there that Mr Bartlett had bought a Schooner called the *Indian Queen* which was lying at Brooklyn, New York to be refitted for a voyage to Africa, and he wanted me to go to New-York that night after her. My first job then was to get a mate to go with me, and on looking around I found that my friend and shipmate William Lloyd [whom Strickland kept in touch with until Lloyd's death in Brookline, Massachusetts in 1911] was available for that purpose. For a crew we had four Kroomen who had lately arrived from Africa as "assistants" in the Barque *D. Godfrey*. These were not good sailors but they were accustomed to vessels and a sea-life and it was thought we might get along with them. We all started with Mr Brooks, Mr Bartletts [sic] bookkeeper to go to New York that evening by the Fall River Line, the Kroomen having a deck passage on the steamer while the rest of us occupied Staterooms. Nothing remarkable occurred until morning, when as the Steamer approached New York and we went to muster our Kroomen we found them surrounded by a crowd of American negroes who were dreadfully excited because as they pretended to imagine we were taking the Kroomen to the seat of war in order to make Soldiers of them. The Kroomen were dreadfully frightened at the negroes because of the way they acted but Mr Brooks told them not to be afraid for he would see to it that the negroes were "taken care of" and leaving the mate and myself at the wharf to reassure the Kroomen he went off and made arrangements with the Officers of the boat to have a policeman at the wharf when the boat arrived to take charge of the situation. The negroes in the meantime had worked themselves into a frenzy over the Kroomen, but the moment the Steamer touched the wharf an energetic policeman came aboard and without ceremony pitched into the negroes, hustling them right and left and not seeming to care how much he hurt them. In the amidst of the melee, Mr Brooks leading the way we all went ashore and struck for the Brooklyn Ferry as fast as we could walk for fear the negroes might follow us. They did not however being occupied by the policeman, but as the Kroomen in their fright actually clung to Mr Brooks whom they knew well and had confidence in going down Broadway although it was early in the morning we presented a most ludicrous appearance. When we arrived in Brooklyn and had found the vessel which was in a very retired place where there was not much going on, the Kroomen regained their Spirits and soon appeared quite at home on board the Schooner. Mr Brooks returned to Boston, and I found myself again with the responsibility of a vessel on my hands and under very peculiar circumstances.[7]

What a story these Kru would have to relate to their brothers and sisters back in the old country about the manner in which their African-American brothers greeted them!

Capt. Peter Strickland found it just and natural to use Africans on his sailing crews. In 1878, Strickland confirms in a letter from Guinea Bissau that Africans operate the vessels he uses for the African trade. "I shall never think of sailing a vessel here with white men."[8] The following year, from the Guinea Bissau coastal town of Bulama, Strickland recommended an African as a superior pilot. "My new pilot Ben-War has about the best reputation of any black Captain on the Coast."[9]

Strickland does not drink, and abhors that conduct in others when taken to excess. He witnesses episodes of intoxication among crews. In Copenhagen in 1859,

Part of the men had gone ashore after breakfast, and soon after dinner one of them came on board intoxicated behaving as sailors usually do when in that condition, and shortly after two others came off in a boat they had hired, but very soon attempted to go ashore again in the same boat. I made an effort to stop them by casting the boat adrift but they were too quick for me and got off using insolent language while some who were lef[t] on deck showed knives as if in defiance. I finally had to get my revolver which had an effect to keep them at bay, although I heard threats from the farthest of them that they would have to kill me, which in the drunken state they were in I knew they would not shrink from doing if I should give them a chance.[10]

Strickland would refer often to his crews as consisting of "half-drunken reprobates," "desperate, sinister-looking vagabonds," and, at their worst, "thugs and murderers." Strickland had to be on his guard; he carried a revolver, but was not known to have used it.

As Strickland knew all too well, intoxication on shipboard was not limited to the crew. On Christmas Day in 1860, Strickland "took direction and guided the vessel down the river to Buenos Aires, as both Capt. Baker and the port pilot were unconscious from the influence of some kind of liquor."[11] Not only did Strickland condemn drinking; he felt obliged to monitor his captain's conduct and be prepared to take over when necessary.

Strickland adapted to a variety of behaviors on the part of the shipmaster or captain. In 1859, he compared two of them. "Our captain is not cautious in the extreme like Captain Baker of the *Mary E. Dunworth,* but is bold almost to recklessness and bound to make time if it can be made. His name is Howe[s], and he belongs in Chatham on Cape Cod."[12] The afore-mentioned Captain Baker, Strickland wrote, would keep all sails close-reefed just in case a "norther" wind might come up. He saw each of these cases as being excessive behavior he would not emulate.

Peter Strickland as a seaman and mate was a careful observer of sea captains' behavior, using these opportunities to weigh what he might do were he at the helm. In 1860, he served under a captain who would work the sailors three extra hours a day. Captain Baker's "plan to keep all hands on deck every afternoon from the time they get dinner until six o'clock to work keeps a sailor fifteen hours out of every twenty-four in the service of the ship is certainly not right, and I would stop the practice everywhere I could."[13]

In one incident, Strickland felt strongly enough about an order to openly challenge his captain. Again, the situation involved alcohol.

Today I had a fracas with the captain which I saw no way to avoid although I should have liked very much to have done so. It came about as follows. When we were near the Equator, and the passenger was I am sure treating him [to liquor], I incautiously perhaps but in the most respectful manner revealed to him my preference for enjoying some leisure in my afternoon watch below which I am sure he has brooded on since, and now that he is under the influence of liquor again he is inclined to reopen the subject, and perhaps to attempt to punish me for it. At any rate when the work which I was directing began he ordered me to go on the stage and go to painting with the men, which I instantly declined to do, because I knew that it would never due [sic] for me to submit to such a degradation proposed to me by a half-drunken man. He then ordered me "to my room," which order I obeyed with alacrity because it did not necessarily involve a degradation and it gave me time to reflect on what I ought to do next. It was then approaching night, and as soon as the time came for me to relieve the Second Mate I went boldly on deck and relieved him. I think this action of mine pretty much sobered the half intoxicated captain who after taking time to reflect followed me on deck with his revolver possibly in his pocket and asked me in a not excited tone of voice why I was not obeying his orders to "keep my room." I replied firmly and with some emphasis, that I was keeping my watch because I knew that the lives of those in the ship and the safety of the property on board of her depended on my doing so! The captain of course knew at once that I was alluding to his habits of intoxication and realizing probably that I could prove what I said and that no court would be apt to sustain him under the circumstances he soon became completely mollified, and at length told me that I might not only go on keeping my watches as usual but that I need not keep on deck when it was my turn to remain below. I thus gained a complete victory but it did not make me feel at all elated.[14]

This incident shows a young officer unafraid to challenge a captain concerning an order. Strickland knew he was in the right and that if ever his behavior were to lead to a courtroom proceeding he would be vindicated. Nevertheless, any victory would seem hollow to the young man, concerned as he was about the captain's weakness for drink and its potential impact on the safety of a vessel, its crew, and passengers.

In a second case, Strickland challenged the same captain in a less direct way, over breaking the Sabbath. In 1857, Strickland would spend his Sundays on board his vessel in meditation and prayer. He would resist attempts by a captain to organize work on Sundays.

> Today the Captain asked the Chief Mate whose name was Wilby to propose to the crew that if they would get the trestle trees up on Sunday he would pay them well for it. There was no necessity for this, and I used what influence I could among my former comrades to induce them to reject the proposition, as I personally did not wish to see such a policy inaugurated. I even prayed that if it was consistent with the Divine Will the Captains mind in this matter might be changed, and at any rate in the course of the day he gave up his idea telling the mate to "never mind it."[15]

No wood was loaded on Sunday. Despite his relatively tender age, Strickland strongly believed in respecting the Sabbath.

Some sailors would wind up in prison. Strickland once sailed from Hamburg to Montevideo with an obstreperous German crew. In Montevideo, the captain called in the army. "The captain was back again with a squad of powerfully built soldiers, armed with bayonets and provided with manacles. All the men but one, the Norwegian, were without ceremony clapped in irons and taken off to prison."[16] Strickland checked to see that his revolver was "in good trim." A Yankee was assigned to replace the German chief mate. The danger of the merchant marine profession included interpersonal violence, as well as threats from the wind and wave.

In April 1857 Strickland assessed his fortunes. He had sailed from Boston to Veracruz, Mexico. The captain gave the crew the option to be discharged there, but Peter decided to continue on to Europe without a stop back home. He justified his decision and looked forward to reaping benefits in the future both in savings and in professional advancement.

> Months must elapse before I shall again be able to visit my native land and see those faces which used to smile on me

sweetly when I returned from school. I am now dealing alone with the great realities of life, and am sensible that I have got to pay well for the most I shall get. Probably if I had elected to take my discharge in Vera Cruz in order to make a visit home I should not now be an officer of a vessel and it might take years even for me to come by as good a chance again. I seem to be giving quite good satisfaction, and even if we go straight home from Hamburgh I am reasonably sure that I shall have at least two months more of experience in making a foreign voyage which in any case will be of utmost importance to me. I am also not spending money, and if this trip shall give me a chance to save the best part of a year's salary that will be a happening which I certainly [will] not feel bad about.[17]

In June 1857 the *Mary E. Dunworth* was in Hamburg, Germany when that city received with great excitement a visit by Czar Alexander II of Russia. Nevertheless, Strickland was overcome by thoughts of home. "Everybody seemed anxious to get a good view of his Imperial Majesty. I did not get a near view but on the whole near enough to suit me, for I would take more pains to see my mother about now than I would all the sovereigns in Europe."[18]

He was feeling pangs of homesickness, this teenager who had embarked on what would be his longest period at sea, sixteen straight months. One can imagine how excited he would be when approaching a port when he might expect mail.

The major question debated politically among Americans in the late 1850s was slavery. While sailing the high seas, Peter Strickland for the most part escaped the slavery debates that took place in the United States; when he returned, he could not ignore them. Despite his exemption from military service, Strickland did not remain aloof. His attitude about the war evolved from abolitionism to one favoring the ending of slavery through compensation to slave owners.

With the north and the south hardening their positions toward slavery in January of 1860, arguments took place on board schooners as well as on land. Hearing such views prompted Peter Strickland to air his own.

This morning a somewhat heated controversy on the Slavery question occurred on board of our ship in which our Captain, the Captain of a large schooner in the Dry dock, the proprietor of the Dry dock who was a Southerner, and a couple more southern gentlemen were the participants. Our Captain was somewhat inclined to the view which favored a continuance of Slavery while the Captain of the Schooner was bitterly, even angrily, opposed to it, while the Southerners were to a man in favor of the southern view. The Southern gentlemen were vociferous against the present attitude of the Republican party North toward them and all said that the most they wanted of the Republicans was to be "Let alone." Our steward, who is a well-feeling black man, listened to the conversation with disgust, and my judgment was that both sides were too much influenced by feeling and that the real truth did not lie in the extreme contentions of either party. I read "Uncle Toms Cabin" soon after it was first published and it affected me considerably, inclining me at first quite strongly in favor of abolitionism, but after much reflection on the subject I at length came to the conclusion that if it were true that the slaves ought to be freed the people of the north ought to bear their share of the burden as well as the people of the south, that the slaves ought to be appraised at their regular market value and the owners compensated for them less their own estimated share in each transaction. From all I can see I judge that this will never be done.[19]

In formulating his view on slavery, Strickland refers to his experience as a northerner having traveled to the south and heard southerners speak on the subject. Yet he sees the problem as national, not regional. He looks toward the federal government to solve the problem with a "buy-out" of slaveholders. He later specifies that the payment should be made from a generalized tax.

In February of 1861, Strickland still clings to his position, but feels that war is close.

It is very likely I think that if the Republican party would at this juncture declare authoritatively that it was in favor of the purchase of all the Slaves by the Government at the going market price, and of freeing them as fast as circumstances and a sound policy would permit, that enough would agree to it to prevent a disruption, but alas, there seems to be no such disposition anywhere at present. The Republican party in charge of the Government is confessedly hostile to Slavery and the South as a consequence is "Secession mad." With those two conditions in the foreground as rampant, what can result but war?[20]

A week later Strickland writes that he cannot bear the thought that his country is to be divided.

At the end of April, Strickland was at sea between Montevideo and New York and did not know that the war had begun with the attack on Fort Sumter more than two weeks earlier. He fears war may already have begun, however, and evokes the possibility of being captured by a privateer. He again hopes for a buy-out of slaveholders and cites the West Indian precedent. He cannot bear to think that his country will wind up in an internal conflict causing loss of life.

If we are to have a Civil War as a result of Mr. Lincoln's election it may have already begun. There was talk of privateers before we left the River, and what if we should be captured by one before we can reach New York. It is not a pleasant subject to think about. . . . How satisfactory it would be if there were now a proposition before the country to settle forever the slavery question by the governments buying all the slaves the way England did in her West India possessions, but there seems to be no one to propose it. It would cost a tremendous sum to be sure, but so will a war if unhappily there is to be one, and it will cost also things much more precious than money.[21]

It was not until May 10, 1861, off Block Island, that Strickland learned that hostilities had commenced between north and south. On that day, the brig *Croton* heading from Rhode Island for Cuba hailed his vessel and excitedly gave the news. Sailing past Staten Island three days later, he saw troops drilling.

Strickland spent much of the war at sea, and some of it along the eastern seaboard as a young merchant officer. In Havana, he saw both northern and southern vessels, as "[t]he Spaniards pride themselves on maintaining strict neutrality 'between the belligerents.'"[22]

Strickland explains in his journal why it was difficult to find a job in the merchant service during the war. For one, American ship owners had to pay a "war-risk," demanded by insurers. Two, since flying an American flag was so troublesome, many owners were selling their vessels abroad. These conditions resulted in many sailors seeking positions and few vessels. At least once, Strickland would find himself captain on board an American vessel flying a British flag to avoid war-risk payments, but he didn't favor that unpatriotic ploy.

On one occasion, his ship barely escaped capture by the Confederate ocean raider, *Alabama*. Stormy weather and the approach of night saved him. On a voyage between Bermuda and Cape Hatteras his vessel was boarded by the U.S. bark *Ethan Allen*, "which was cruising for privateers and blockade-runners."[23]

Strickland never served in the war; nevertheless, he had strong feelings about it. Walking around Boston in January of 1864, he passed a group of young recruits, which made him shudder.

> I went to Boston and in going along Commercial St. passed a squad of recruits who were guarded from running away by a couple of soldiers armed and I suppose detailed for that purpose who would undoubtedly have shot anyone who left the ranks. What a dreadful thing war is, and what humiliations those have to endure who take a part in it. The common soldiers when they have the best of intentions are often treated as if they were felons and criminals, but there don't seem to be any remedy for it under the system. If we go to New Orleans we shall be pretty near to War, so much so possibly as to become affected by it, but I have an antipathy to everything concerning it and hope that in the Providence of God that it will soon be over.[24]

Captain Strickland made his first trip to West Africa during the final year of the Civil War. While he considered himself fortunate to have found a berth during the war, the more he read about voyages to Africa the more he worried about his new destination because of African fevers.

> I spent some time today looking through some of the *Robert Wing's* old Log-Books and found that hitherto she has seldom made a voyage without losing one or more of her crew by sickness, principally what is called African fever. This seems to have been caused by her going to different places in the Rivers along the Coast where malarious [sic] influence is present all the time. I think we are not likely to change ports to much extent on this voyage, and so perhaps we shall be less exposed, and if I find hereafter that the voyages are conducted in a manner to make them dangerous I may feel obliged to leave the trade which is not encouraging to think of.[25]

Strickland visited Gorée Island off the coast of Senegal where they unloaded leaf tobacco and lumber and loaded peanuts and animal hides. In October of the same year, 1864, Strickland was back on the island of Gorée for another cargo of peanuts and hides, plus some cotton: three products sorely needed in the United States due to disruptions from the war. It was his fifteenth transatlantic crossing. He realized that the ship owner, Matthew Bartlett, was considering him for long-term African assignment to replace a Captain Shaw whose health has been ruined on the African coast. He confided in his journal that even if asked, he would resist the offer.

> Arrived at Goree in the morning. 41 days from Boston which is not bad for a passage out, considering the season. When I went ashore in the morning I found Captain Skinner all-right but Captain Shaw of the Sch *Hydrangea* was sick with fever having been on a trip to the rivers in the rainy season. I know that I am wanted to take his place but think I shall decline absolutely if the position is offered to me, no matter what the consequences may be.[26]

Over a decade later, however, Strickland would accept the offer
to live on the African coast and trade for the Bartlett firm. He was
not initially impressed with Gorée, where he would end up living
for a quarter of a century.

The Peter Strickland Collection at Mystic Seaport Library in
Connecticut holds the official journals of Strickland's first voyages
to West Africa in 1864–1866, where he commands the schooner
Indian Queen and the brig *Robert Wing*. The journals contain space
to record the principal data from each twenty-four-hour segment
of the trip: departure time, course, direction and strength of winds,
speed in knots each hour, distance traveled per day, latitude and
longitude, daily weather observations, names of ships spotted,
names of sails taken in or out, when destination first sighted, when
pilot came on board, when anchor let out, arrival time, number of
days during crossing, when unloading and loading of cargo began
and finished, and contents of cargo.

While much of the data would appear fastidious and tedious
to the reader, a judicious condensed selection of items can serve to
convey a flavor of the voyages. In his first voyage to Africa, Peter
Strickland served as chief mate on the *Indian Queen*. The schooner
sailed out of Boston harbor on Sept. 7, 1864, and arrived at Gorée on
Oct. 17, after having passed through Cape Verde Islands to unload
some cargo. The vessel's cargo consisted of leaf tobacco samples,
shingles, apples, milk, oysters, butter, clams, pickles, mackerel, and
codfish. On Oct. 25, a "tornado at night, thunder and lightning and
heavy showers of rain" interrupted the unloading on Gorée. Instead
of picking up a return cargo on Gorée, the vessel was "sold to a
Frenchman of Gorée to be delivered up immediately. Our voyage
may be considered at an end."[27] The journal was signed "Peter
Strickland, New London, Connecticut, USA." Although the *Indian
Queen* was a vessel registered in Boston and belonged to Boston
ship owner Matthew Bartlett, Strickland still considered himself
a Connecticut man. Little by little he would relinquish ties to his
birthplace, in a few years buying property in Boston and settling
his family there.

Strickland captained the brig *Robert Wing* on Aug. 11, 1865, as
it "started in tow of a steamer at 11:00 AM and went out through
Broad Sound" from the port of Boston. On Aug. 13, the vessel sailed

by the Bay of Fundy and entered the Gulf Stream. Aug 18, 21, and 22 saw "squally weather" and Aug. 25 "strong trade winds." On Sept. 4, 1865, the vessel

> [a]t 1.00 AM made the light on Cape de Verde right ahead bearing SSE. Passed Cape Manuel at 8.00 AM and came to an anchor in Gorée about ten o'clock. About 12 heard heavy peals of thunder to the SE and in less than half an hour we were visited by a furious tornado. Let go the second anchor and paid out 60 fathoms chain. The first furious blast was accompanied by a blinding rain rendering almost impossible to look to windward and I was thankful that we were lucky enough to get to an anchor before it came in. Almost all the vessels in the roads dragged their anchors.[28]

On both Sept. 5 and 6, more tornadoes visited the *Robert Wing*. Nevertheless, on the sixth, two men were employed half a day unloading 350 bundles of wood shingles. Discharging ended on Sept. 11; on the 12, a French sloop of war arrived in the Gorée roads. On the 14, the brig set out for St. Louis at the mouth of the Senegal River to the north.

This was Strickland's first trip to St. Louis, the capital city in the French colony of Senegal. He wrote in his ship journal on Sept. 19, 1865, "At 7.00 AM a steamer came out from the river and took us in tow. Crossed the bar and were towed up to St Louis where we arrived about nine o'clock. Came to an anchor below a pontoon bridge that crosses the river abreast of the town." This pontoon bridge, inaugurated in July 1865, was named the Faidherbe Bridge after the French governor of Senegal in the 1850s. In 1897, a solid drawbridge would replace the pontoons.

Until the end of September, the *Robert Wing* unloaded her cargo, in "hot sultry weather" and another tornado. While peanuts were being loaded into the hold, Strickland reports the desertion of one of the crew and the arrest and imprisonment of another for drunkenness. Just as the St. Louis visit was not without incident, so was the vessel's departure on Oct 4. "Got underweigh [sic] in the morning and took hawsers from the steamtug St Louis in order to go over the bar. When the steamer attempted to go ahead of us he struck us on the port side by the fore rigging and smashed a couple of bulwark planks . . . . We crossed the bar safely about 7.00 AM and put to sea. At about 8.00 AM the vessel was struck by a tornado and we were obliged to run before it for an hour close reefed the maintopsail and furled light sails." Struck by tug and tornado, Strickland's vessel made the return trip to Gorée to take on animal hides before departing for Boston. Signing the bills of lading indicating a cargo of hides and peanuts was Capt. Henry O. Skinner, sea captain and West African representative of ship owner Matthew Bartlett. In 1865, Skinner lived in a large house overlooking the port of Gorée. Upon his death fifteen years later, Capt. Peter Strickland would replace him as Bartlett agent and occupy the house, which changed its appellation from the Skinner House to the Strickland House. Strickland lived in the house until 1905.

Again, the voyage is eventful. A crewmember has caught fever. The wind blows a hurricane from the northeast. The following day the "gale still continues with unabated violence. Vessel labors and strains badly shipping large quantities of water." Having left Gorée on Oct. 7, 1865, the *Robert Wing* arrives at the wharf in Boston harbor on Nov. 1. On board are 8,142 bushels of peanuts and 1,000 animal hides, weighing nine thousand pounds.

Strickland's third voyage to West Africa begins from Boston on Jan. 5, 1866. As the brig *Robert Wing* passes the Boston Light at 1:00 PM, the crew discovers a boy from Woonsocket, Rhode Island stowed away in the coalhole. On Jan. 6, snow and ice cover the decks. On the 12th, Strickland reports a "[t]remendous sea threatening to swamp the vessel at times." On Jan. 13, Henry Smart, the cook from Bristol, England, falls overboard and is never seen again. The crossing from Boston to Gorée takes twenty-eight days. Their best day is Jan. 6, when they travel 215 miles; their worst Jan. 20, when all they make is sixteen miles in the day.

The early days in February are spent unloading tubs of leaf tobacco, bundles of sawed pine shingles, and barrels of rum. Just as the *Robert Wing* prepares for departure on Feb. 14th at 3:00 PM, a French brig named *Louis the 14th* backs into her "while trying to get underweigh and shove in the topgallant bulwarks."

The later days of February find the *Robert Wing* unloading tobacco and white pine shipping boards in St. Louis and taking on gum and peanuts. Departure from St. Louis on Feb. 30 is out of the question, as tornado weather and heavy surf along the coast make it impossible for a steamtug to tow the *Robert Wing* over the bar. They wait six days for favorable weather. On March 4, the steamtug is able to guide the brig over the bar and out to sea for the return trip to Gorée. They take in some cotton, sail to Rufisque to pick up more peanuts, and then depart for Boston.

The first three voyages Strickland made to Africa—among the dozens he would make—clearly convey the nature of a sea captain's life: busy, dangerous, and fraught with one difficulty after another; tornadoes and hurricanes; crew desertions and imprisonments; stowaways and men overboard; ramming accidents with other vessels; and African fever. Underlying each merchant voyage is the captain's responsibility to securely load and unload the cargo.

To remain fit to meet and overcome all such challenges, a sailor had to be careful with his health, not an easy feat in tropical Africa over a century ago. Fortunately, Peter Strickland's upbringing included—besides strong religious beliefs and firm educational principles—an awareness of good health and nutrition.

Peter would bring on shipboard items for his comfort, such as a mattress. He made it himself from cornhusks, which he collected in New London during the month of October. He practiced an ingenious system for protecting himself from the heat and mosquitoes when traveling in warm climates. While off the coast of Havana with a load of Canadian spruce boards, he explains the strategy.

> It is almost impossible to sleep well in the early part of the nights on account of the heat and mosquitoes. I do not attempt to sleep in a Stateroom, but take some light sail like a royal, and suspend it like a table cloth by tying four little chunks of wood on the underneath side, to which I attach cords made fast to objects high enough above the deck to keep the part of the sail which forms the top of the sleeping apartment suspended at the distance of a little more than a yard. Into this tent-like structure I introduce the narrow mattress which at sea fits my berth and make up my bed top of it. The night air on the outside of this tent assisted to keep it cool and I managed to sleep some in it better than I could

have slept below, but of course the ventilation was poor, or rather there was no ventilation and I did not enjoy it.[29]

During his sailing days, Strickland reports bouts with malaria, influenza, dengue fever, and sciatica. His first episode with malaria was in Veracruz, Mexico. He felt "fever and ague." "The captain mixed me up about half a tumbler of Castor-Oil with peppermint, a pretty stiff dose, but I took it without flinching as I was anxious to get the malarial poison out of my system as soon as I could."[30] Two days later, he started taking quinine. After three days, the fever had left him. Strickland then "took salts" to supplement the quinine.

Once Strickland settles into life in the French colony of Senegal, he is exposed to cycles of epidemics, which ravage the territory. When smallpox hits the cities of Dakar, Gorée, and Rufisque in 1895, he notes that many people are not vaccinated. Strickland wisely goes to the hospital for a vaccination. Typhoid fever struck Senegal the same year.

Peter Strickland paid careful attention to what he ate. On his own in Africa, he made sure to maintain a healthy diet, but on shipboard, he had little choice. Sailors depended on coffee, and Strickland found their brew seriously lacking. In 1859, he noted, "In the morning I drank a cup of coffee, or what passes for Coffee, which for some reason did not agree with me. I felt quite ill from the effects of it. Towards night however I felt better. The Coffee that is given sailors is a cheap manufactured article with probably but very little pure coffee in it."[31] Later, when Strickland had settled in West Africa, he recorded his favorite recipe for a delicious coffee blend: fifty percent from Rio Nuñez, Guinea, and fifty percent from the island of Fogo in the Cape Verde Islands.

Strickland recognized that a seaman's diet was generally unhealthy. As captain, he pointed out the deficiencies he saw, although he does not mention any steps he took to correct them.

I am convinced from many things I have read and also from experience that the ordinary food given sailors in the most of our large ships and in some of the smaller ones such as salt meats and biscuits is not only more or less unwholesome but in most cases positively injurious, and it is I think not surprising that in spite of the good air and healthy exercise that seamen on most voyages have they are much subject to constipation, boils and fever which they would not be if they were provided with a more healthful diet.[32]

Already at age twenty, Strickland was showing signs of maturity, weighing his current circumstances and finding favorable elements which would help him endure long absences from his loved ones. Strickland often marked his birthday and Christmas Day with a special journal entry. On Christmas Day in 1857, his ship was in Buenos Aires harbor in Argentina. He wrote, "This is Christmas day even here, and while my good friends at home are enjoying their turkeys and geese with accessories I have nothing but the usual fresh beef and ostrich eggs. It is however possible that I am enjoying what I have as much as they do what they have. Happiness lies more in the way people are constituted than it does in their circumstances and conditions."[33]

Strickland was convinced of the benefit of eating fresh fruit. "We received a large quantity of fruit by the *Magellan*: grapes, pears, melons & apples. These things are very dear, but there is no doubt that they assist powerfully to preserve the health."[34] Careful all his life of what he spent, Strickland was willing to splurge for healthy fruit. Later, he kept track of the arrival of steamers from France such as the *Magellan* to be there when fresh produce arrived in West Africa.

Captain Strickland tried to care for his health while at sea. His eyes suffered from ocean glare. On a merchant trip to New Orleans at the age of twenty-one, he procured for himself his first pair of glasses, with green protective lenses. He noted that while studying Latin his eyes would hurt. Strickland also got a boil on a finger, he thought from drinking the brackish water the ship took on board in Stockholm harbor. He often damaged fingers and nails from handling the rigging.

Strickland was aware of the sickness he suffered due to handling goatskins in preparation for export. Goat hides were a principal object of import into the United States from West Africa, particularly during and after the Civil War when leather for shoes and boots was hard to come by. To prevent rotting, hides were sprayed with arsenic before transatlantic shipment. Handling the treated hides often made one sick; Strickland and his crew experienced it often. As the hide cargo was often accompanied by bags of shelled peanuts, the arsenic may also have affected the nuts during the crossing.

> Probably poisoned hides in the cargo had much to do with my feeling of illness, for the fumes from the hides can be detected in the cabin when the vessel first leaves port but later when they become settled an odor is not noticeable. Our peanuts are stowed with the hides and must be more or less affected with the arsenic that forms the basis of the Hide poison and yet people eat the peanuts both in their raw state and when used in confectionary. If people could always know the history of the "nice things" which are given them to eat I think we should see some wry faces made.[35]

Strickland suffered from chronic catarrh most of his adult life. This malady gave him symptoms of a hot forehead and pressure on the head. He sensed an inflammation between the eyes, causing vertigo.

Only one letter that Peter wrote his mother has survived. Peter wrote her from Bissau in 1876 and included a paragraph on his health, a topic of concern to every mother. One earlier reference in Strickland's journal includes the fact that Peter's mother did not think much of her son living so far away in Africa. In this summary of his health, he does not allude to the grave diseases common in the tropics.

> My health seems excellent now, and I am very comfortably situated, much better than I should be at sea. I have plenty to eat, plenty to drink, and a plenty to do, and the hard times of which so many complain don't affect me a particle. . . . It doubtless seems a terrible thing to you to be living out in Africa among panthers, crocodiles, and such things, and where just a sniff of the unwholesome air is supposed to be sure death to white people, but I can assure Nature is just as pleasant here as at home, and the weather far less changeable. My catarrh troubles me far less here than in

Boston, and I think on the whole my health is just as good every way.[36]

The upbeat tone of the letter must have been music to the ears of Laura White Strickland, who received this letter when she was sixty-eight years old and recently widowed. She would have had difficulty picturing her sailor son's physical environs. He had promised her that each time he returned to his home country he would come to see her, and he did everything he could to respect his promise. Short of a personal visit, a letter would help a great deal to reassure his mother that his health was even better than it was at sea, and better than when he lived in New England.

One Peter Strickland letter gives his normal daily menu, an indication of his healthy diet when he was on his own and not on shipboard.

Let me tell you how I am living here, which, though not quite correct, may come as a useful lesson to you, and perhaps do you much good. I cannot get any bread only of the Baker, and of him I take two small loaves each morning, and an old black woman brings me a wine-bol [sic] the full of milk. With one loaf of the Bread, the milk, and some bananas, guavas, or oranges. I take a lunch every morning at half past seven (you see my breakfast requires no cooking). I have Breakfast generally at eleven, a fresh fish, potatoes & onions. At 6:00 PM I have Dinner. Vegetable soup flavored sometimes with Beef or Chicken, then Greens garnished round with Eggs, then Peas, then Rice, on which for the want of Molasses I use a little Honey. I also consume my other Loaf of Bread with Butter in the Course of the Day. If any grease is required for cooking it is so little that at present I use butter and olive oil. . . . Sugar I do not use half a pound of it in a month. . . . I keep a large tub in the room adjoining the one where I sleep, into which the Cook turns a kettle of hot water at supper-time, so that it cools just right for my bath when I retire at 8:00 PM. So you see my habits are very simple and inexpensive. . . . My living now does not cost me over twenty-five cents a day. . . . I have not drunk a bottle of wine since I arrived here.[37]

Fresh fish; fresh fruit and vegetables; greens; little sugar; barely any grease; no cakes or pies; no alcohol: in sum, an extremely healthy diet. Manifesting temperance and economy, his beneficial diet was one more sign of the man's good judgment, helping him lead a long life.

Strickland weighed himself regularly and entered the figure in his journal. The weight varied between 174 and 194. It is not known how tall he was, except that he was less than six feet. One time he began to enter his height in his journal: for feet, he wrote "5." When it came to the inches, he left a blank.

Weighing himself would lead him to comment on how he should take off pounds.

"Was a little surprised today to find myself weigh 189 lbs net. I do not seem to myself to be very fat, but I am nevertheless conscious of a slightly uncomfortable sense of fullness and weight. I am sure I should feel better to weigh only about 175, or perhaps 170 would be better. I mean to reduce myself to the first of these figures and try that a spell and after perhaps I will try the other. If I had more exercise this would be easy but it is not so easy to do it by diet alone."[38]

Even a healthy sailor on the Atlantic was often no match for the elements. Many of Strickland's voyages took place in the North Atlantic, notorious for its dangers due to extreme wind, ice, and fog. In his fifty-three years on ocean-going vessels, he experienced his share of narrow escapes.

Strickland's closest call came on an early transatlantic voyage near where the *Titanic* would sink. In 1916, he looked back on the scary event.

On the 6th of September 1866, just fifty years ago I was on board the Brig *Robert Wing* in a hurricane not far from the place where the *Titanic* went down. We were then in almost equal danger, but cutting away the masts relieved the pressure of the wind against them and saved us. Every time the date comes round I remember the occurrence with gratitude that we then escaped the danger.[39]

Strickland took note of other North Atlantic accidents. On July 4, 1898, the steamship *Bourgogne* of the French Line went down after a collision with the British steel sailing vessel *Cromartyshire* off Sable Island, Nova Scotia. Neither iceberg nor hurricane was to blame, but another menace in the North Atlantic, heavy fog. In August 1898 he wrote the *Boston Transcript* to argue for an international agreement.

> Now that the sea-sick passenger has been interviewed and the "arm-chair" critics have all had their say as to the cause of the terrible disaster which happened to the *Bourgogne*, is it not time to get to something practical, with a view to reduce to a minimum the danger of meeting with such accidents in the future? The rule to avoid such accidents is simple, easy to apply, and if adopted would add much to the comfort and pleasure of passengers by diminishing their apprehension of danger. . . fogs dangerous to navigation but rarely occur outside the 200 fathom line of Soundings. If then all passenger Steamers on their passages across either way were strictly forbidden by international agreement ever to come within the 200 fathom line of Soundings until their American port should bear northwest, the danger distance would be reduced from more than 200 miles to less than 200, and the liability of being dashed in pieces by ice-bergs or of meeting with collisions would be diminished as much as 90 percent.
>
> From my point of view, (and I have crossed the Atlantic more than a hundred times in charge of a vessel) there is no blame to be attached to any-one belonging to the French line because of the accident to the *Bourgogne*. The Great Public wants quick passages at cheap rates, and has been content to take the risk of its safety from the mode of navigation that has been practiced: because, after all, serious accidents have been the exception and not the rule. The Great Public can have more safety if it wants it by insisting that the Steamers on which they take passage shall be navigated only in deep water, where fogs never prevail, and that on leaving port they shall always take the most direct course to such deep

water. The only drawback to this would be that it might add a very few hours to the length of each passage. . . . It is a crying injustice to Steamship Commanders that they are given so much of discretion in navigating their ships when so much is expected of them.

It seems to me that all Steamers which carry passengers between America and Europe and vice versa should be required by law to pass all the banks in not less than 200 fathoms of water, and to make for that depth as soon as possible after leaving port on each side.[40]

Strickland followed the affair closely in the press, and noted in his journal that the

Halifax Court of Inquiry in its report concerning the causes of the disaster to the *Bourgogne* has advocated a similar route, and now that the matter is fresh in the public mind it would seem that if the subject is pressed in quarters where the means for action lie, that something effectual may soon be done to render the lives of passengers safer in future. But while I perfectly agree with the decision of the Court in recommending a more southern route for Steamers, I must beg to dissent from its opinion in attaching Special blame to Captain Deloncle because the disaster occurred to his vessel a few miles north of the route usually adopted by Steamers of the Company.[41]

While defending the captain of the *Bourgogne*, Strickland cheered the fact that a court shared his views on a more southerly route.

In retirement, Strickland heard at his home in Dorchester, Massachusetts about the sinking of the *Titanic* on April 12, 1912. Fourteen years after the *Bourgogne*'s sinking, the extreme dangers of North Atlantic voyages were unabated.

The dreadful news came today by "Wireless" from New-foundland that the *Titanic* sank before help could arrive to her and that about 1300 people went down with the ship while a little less than 900, mostly women, were saved by the ships boats. This is indeed dreadful news, and it is possible that after it Steamers will be compelled to go further south, at least during the worst months of floating ice.[42]

Capt. Peter Strickland would report shipwrecks within his consular jurisdiction in West Africa, but he never was victim to a sinking, shipwreck, or major collision. However, he did get lost in a terrible fog north of Boston, and he reported almost falling overboard. On Christmas Day, 1859, Strickland threw a rope to a sailor who had fallen overboard and saved him.[43] The combination of risks inherent to the job and unhealthy mariner life prompted Strickland to pick up his pen on behalf of sailors.

Before examining in the next chapter the book Strickland wrote, however, let us put together a list of the vessels the captain mentions in his correspondence, journal, and dispatches from 1857 until 1905. Where known, the voyage years are marked. In the early vessels, Strickland served as second mate and chief mate. In many, he was shipmaster. In a few toward the end, he traveled as passenger. This list follows an earlier one Strickland himself gave, at the outset of this chapter, of his first consecutive twenty-seven sailing vessels.

Table 2. Partial List of Vessels Strickland Sailed in, 1859–1905

Type	Vessel	Year
	Avala	1859
	Humphrey Purinton	1859
	Richard Alsop	1860
Bark	Tremont	1863
Schooner	Benjamin Willis	1863
Brig	Robert Wing	1864
Schooner	Hydrangea	1864
Schooner	Sarah Jane	1864
Bark	Rapid	1867–70
Bark	Zingarella	1870–82
Schooner	Gazelle	1878
	Mary Allerton	1879
	Mary Joof	1879
	Ida Blanche	1879–80
	Sulivan	1880–98?
	Jennie Diverty	
	Arthur Egglers	
	E. H. Yarrington	
	Daniel Webster	
	Warren Hellett	
	Elm	
	Chicopee	
	Candace	
	J. H. Ward	
Bark	Jennie Cushman	1883–86
Schooner	Ripple	1884
Brig	Lucy W. Snow	1884–85
Steamer	Lancaster	1885
Packet	Congo	1885
Schooner	M. E. Higgins	1888
Steamer	Normandie	1888
	Waldemar	1889
	Mejunticook	1890
	Scythia	1890
Schooner	Rebecca L. Evans	1895
Bark	Charles F. Ward	1897
Schooner	H. E. Thomsen	1898
Schooner	Oliver Cromwell	1899
Steamer	Jeanette Waemann	1902
Schooner	Unique	1902
Schooner	New England	1903
Steamer	Mayflower	1903
Steamer	Chili	1903
	Angola	1903
Schooner	Jeanne Lippitt	1903
Schooner	Herald of the Morning	1904
Schooner	Levi S. Andrews	1904
Steamer	Atlantique	1905
Steamer	RMS Republic	1905
Steamer	La Cordillère	1905

1. His only known portrait, Peter Strickland sent this picture along with an autobiographical sketch to New York in 1898. A handsome man sporting a Mark Twain-style mustache, he complained in his journal about the inappropriate custom of formal dress in the tropics.

2. This two-chimney center-hall Georgian colonial farmhouse, built around 1760 in the Quaker Hill section of New London, belonged to three generations of Peter Stricklands. Capt. Strickland's father was one of four family members who inherited the house. He lived in it until 1833.

3. Capt. Peter Strickland purchased this wood-frame house in Dorchester in 1871 for his young family. Strickland enjoyed watching the movements of ships, using his spyglass mounted on the back of the house. This is the home Strickland returned to each time leave was granted from his consular duties and to which he retired in 1905.

4. Built in about 1840 overlooking Gorée port, the two contiguous buildings making up the residence and consulate that Peter Strickland leased from 1880 until 1905 are still standing. Then the exterior was whitewashed; now it is painted crimson and ochre.

5.   An unidentified correspondent in Boston sent this envelope to Capt. Peter Strickland. Five postmarks on both sides of the envelope attest to its itinerary: Boston, August 2; Paris, August 11; Bordeaux, August 12; Marseille, August 13; and Gorée August 22. Twenty days in 1889: sometimes it takes as long today!

6.   Another envelope sent to the sea captain shows three modern attributes: a preprinted stamp, a preprinted return address, and a typewritten address. Postmarks on both sides reveal that the postal journey began April 4 and ended May 6. Strickland served as agent for the Luckett-Wake Tobacco Company.

January 1857

1

___Thurs 1___

This day is indeed one of the pleasantest I ever saw.—The heavy trade-wind clouds rising astern,— the blue sky overhead,—and the long undulating swell with an occasional break at the top of each mighty wave, form a picture which the most ambitious painter might choose for his art with but scant hope of doing it complete justice.—

About 8.00 a.m. a large Grampus came playing around the quarter, but we did not disturb him.—

At noon we were in Lat 22°.49′ N.—Long 47°.54 West.—

___Frid 2___

Lat at noon 22°.23′ N :—Long 48°.05′ West.— The weather being pleasant during the day we unbent the main-topsail and put some new Cringles in the leeches.—In the course of the night the wind hauled so much to the southward that we were obliged to take in the studdingsails and brace the yards to sail sharp by the wind.—The wind also breezed up so fresh that we took in the royals and topgallantsails, but this was hardly necessary, as the increase in the wind proved of short duration;—the breeze died away and we had the weather calm and rainy the rest of the night.—

___Sat 3___

Lat at noon 22°.23′ N.—The weather we have just had was an interruption of what is usual in the region of the trade winds at this season, and may have been caused by the influence of a "Norther" to the northward of the tropic of Cancer.—These strong winds not infrequently in the winter penetrate far down towards the Equator, and if they cannot much change the climate after passing the latitude of 25°, they at least interrupt the usual order of things for a short period.—

188915

7. At age nineteen, Strickland left Boston for England on a merchant sailing vessel to bring coal and iron to Mexico, and started to record his life adventures and reflections. This is the first of 2,500 journal pages he left from 1857 until 1921, a sixty-four-year span. Many volumes of the journal are missing, however.

JOURNAL OF VOYAGES

Of the *Indian Queen*

Robert Wing

Commanded by *Peter Strickland*

Kept by

NAVIGATION STORE,

Sign of Mercury and the Quadrant,

No. 126, COMMERCIAL, CORNER OF RICHMOND STREET,

BOSTON,

F. W. LINCOLN, JR., & CO.

Sextants, Quadrants, Barometers, Thermometers, Spy-Glasses,

LOG-GLASSES, BINNACLES, AND COMPASSES,

Constantly on hand, and repaired at the lowest rates.

NAUTICAL INSTRUMENTS, CHARTS, AND BOOKS.

8.   Cover page of the log book kept by Peter Strickland on his first three voyages to West Africa in the schooner *Indian Queen* and the brig *Robert Wing*. He commanded these vessels in 1864–1866 from Boston to Gorée and back.

[Form No. 37.]   9

CONSULATE OF THE UNITED STATES OF AMERICA.

MARINE NOTE OF PROTEST.

Port of *Goree - Dakar*

On this *Eighth* day of *April*, in the year of our Lord eighteen hundred and *Eighty-six*, before me, *Peter Strickland* Consul of the United States of America for *Goree - Dakar* and the dependencies thereof, personally appeared *George Strickland*, Master of the Ship or Vessel called the *M E Higgins* of *Boston*, Mass of the burden of *89.76* Tons, or thereabouts, and declared that on the *31st* day of *March* last past he sailed in and with the said ship from the port of *Bissau* laden with *African Produce*, and arrived in the said ship at *Goree* on *April 8th 1886* and having experienced boisterous and tempestuous weather on the voyage,

hereby enters this Note of Protest accordingly, to serve and avail him hereafter if found necessary.

Attested:

George Strickland.
Master.

Peter Strickland
U. S. Consul.

9.   This April 8, 1886, protest follows a voyage of the schooner *M. E. Higgins* that had met bad weather. The consul is Peter Strickland; the shipmaster, his son George Strickland. In 1888, George drowned accidentally after falling from the railing of the same vessel.

3

Author from Boston

Dr Strickland

In his leisure time on board ship, Peter Strickland did not carve scrimshaw; he wrote a book. In 1873, A. Williams & Co. in Boston published *A Voice from the Deep* by "Capt. P. Strickland." It was an ambitious undertaking for a man who had left school at age fifteen. We know he was a compulsive writer, but penning a daily entry in a journal is not the same as developing and presenting a book-length treatise. After twenty years as a sailor, carefully noting the injustices in a mariner's life, Strickland could no longer keep his strong convictions to himself.

We do not know how Strickland managed the financing of the handsome 189-page book with a nautical design gilt-stamped on the cover. Nor is it known how he chose his publisher. A. Williams & Co. produced a dozen books in the 1870s on a variety of topics: religious sermons, monographs of military figures, town histories, and tourist guides. Of these topics, only religious sermons have a connection with Strickland. Throughout the 1860s when visiting Boston, Strickland attended church services led by Reverend Edward Thompson Taylor. A sailor who became a preacher, "Father Taylor" preached to sailors and tried to help them. Taylor may have provided Strickland contacts in the publishing world.

There are only two references in Strickland's writings to the book: one from a diplomatic dispatch in 1889 and the other from a 1912 journal entry almost forty years after the book was printed.

In the first reference, Peter Strickland was writing to the assistant secretary of state in mid-1889. The recent election of Benjamin Harrison had given Strickland hopes that the newly elected president would "restore to America her nearly lost foreign commerce." Strickland announced to the State Department that "Years ago when a young shipmaster and therefore keenly interested in everything which relates to vessels, noting the rapid decline in the ship-owning interest which in many ways affected me, and about the wretched condition of seamen with whom I was constantly having dealings I, in moments of leisure at Sea, wrote the enclosed book entitled 'A Voice from the Deep,' which bears on the subject."[1]

Strickland had already been a consul for five years when he enclosed a copy of his book along with a dispatch to the State Department. He could have provided a copy of his book much earlier, when the Department was considering his name for the consular position in West Africa. Strickland did not actively seek out the job: the State Department suggested he take on the position. Strickland chose to send his book to Washington when an American President had just been elected who might try to revive American shipping abroad, notably in Africa. This was a thesis dear to Strickland's heart. Captain Strickland also recognized that the "wretched condition" of seamen was the overriding norm and he believed that a sympathetic national government might take steps to remedy this situation.

The second reference to his book was from a journal entry in Dorchester in early 1912, when a schoolteacher dropped in on the Strickland household after church one day and left a calendar.

> I presented her [Miss Breed] at the same time with a copy of my Book entitled "A Voice from the Deep" which I think she will appreciate. I wrote this Book the same as Crusoe built his Canoe, without much thought how I was going to "launch it." I also in writing it paid no attention to people's prejudices, and perhaps erred in making some statements which needed more explanation than I at the time gave them in order to give the exact impression I meant to convey. I can see now that many good people might object to remarks made about our Custom-House as they at that time affected Sailors. I wrote however from my own experience and have nothing in substance to take back, although I can now see that I might have made a better impression if I had studied more in penning my manuscript to avoid misconstruction.[2]

Almost forty years after publication, Strickland still had copies of his book in his home to give to visitors. Today, copies can be found on shelves of several university libraries, maritime research centers, and a few antique book dealers.

The book lacks subtlety: it is verbose and exaggerated, stating and restating its thesis. On the title page appears a political cartoon; at the end of the volume, a poem. References to the Almighty and the Master's kingdom permeate the book. However, the underlying thesis is clear: sailors are getting a raw deal and something should be done about it.

In the cartoon image, two sailors have fallen overboard. As they struggle to survive on a plank of wood, a voice wafts from the departing full-rigged ship, "Can't stop! Time is money!"[3] The cartoon on the title page is reproduced in the gilt stamp on the book cover. The cartoon dramatizes the callous neglect with which ship owners, the government, and the public treat sailors.

In his "Prefatory Remarks," Peter Strickland establishes his authority to write such a book. "The author of this little volume has been a sailor for nearly twenty years. He has, in that time, served in nearly every capacity on board of a merchant-ship."[4] Although few readers would have heard of the author, his credentials give him utmost credibility.

Strickland confesses that he has long been appalled by the miserable condition of seamen. For years it never occurred to him to try to do anything much about it. Strickland recognized that he was no public speaker. Realizing this limitation and demonstrating considerable pluck to persevere, he made a decision to write a treatise, despite his literary shortcomings.

I had no means of gaining the public ear. As to lecturing, that was entirely out of the question; for I had never yet been prevailed upon to speak a dozen sentences before an audience on any one subject in my life. Writing would do better, for me at least; but then I very well know that my seafaring live had never been favorable for developing such habits of thinking, and modes of expression, as would qualify me to produce any thing like a perfect literary performance. The rules of grammar had partially fled from my memory; and I had had but little occasion to submit my mind to the vigorous discipline which is so essential to give even genius any well-grounded hope of achieving success as an author.[5]

After closely observing American sailors from several perspectives over two decades, Strickland concludes that they are condemned to a life of misery, loneliness, and depravity. Moreover, no one cared.

The author develops his case by identifying the sailor's five malefactors: shipping agents, ship owners, boarding masters, ship officers, and consuls.

Shipping agents:

The brokers employed to hire seamen, called shipping-agents or shipping-masters, frequently exercise a very bad influence upon them by the methods which many of them adopt to get crews, and by cheating in various ways. These brokers frequently have authority from owners to pay off some of the crews they have shipped; and in such case figures (which won't lie) are often so arranged as to tell tales which make poor Jack's heart ache. Sometimes, again, when men are plenty, and chance scarce, they will extort a fee from the sailor, besides the regular brokerage which they get from the shipowner.[6]

Ship owners:

Some shipowners connive at and even encourage the unlawful discharge of seamen at foreign ports, where cheaper help can be obtained. . . . Shipowners are responsible for not providing suitable accommodations on board of their vessels for sailors, and also for not supplying them with a sufficient quantity of good wholesome food and water.[7]

Boarding-masters:

Boarding-masters that have a parcel of drunken swabs on hand, that they consider in debt to them, will sometimes pay liberally to get them shipped off; and that, too, is one reason why good ships are so often cursed with bad crews.[8]

Ship officers:

There are also several direct agencies for evil existing on board of many of our ships; and perhaps we cannot do better than to introduce a few of them here. One is the most debasing, shameless, and heartless tyranny. Some men are natural tyrants in the worst sense of the word; and when poor Jack gets into a ship where one of these fiends holds sway, his condition is indeed deplorable. The worst kind of slavery is an enviable state compared with the usage on board of these "hells afloat," as the sailors call them. The men are beaten with belaying-pins, knocked down with brass knuckles, kicked with heavy boots, deprived of sleep, and tortured in almost every possible way to satisfy the fiendish malice of those monsters of depravity, who delight and glory in being called fighting men, bullies, and horses.[9]

Consuls:

Another thing which goes to prove to seamen that landsmen are sharks and hypocrites is the treatment which they often receive at the hands of some of our foreign consuls. Some of these officials are humane, well educated, and intelligent, and perhaps every way worthy of the position they have attempted to fill; but it is to be feared there are many among them who are inclined to seek their own instead of another's wealth. Broken-down merchants that have failed in business, and who, perhaps, were never burdened with honesty, will sometimes contrive to get a number of respectable names attached to their petitions to the government for an office which will give them a good living, a respectable position in society, and, at the same time, remove them as far as possible from the scene of their former mishaps; and they are very apt to succeed. Many of these men know and care but very little about the rights or the wrongs of seamen, but have an eye continually to replenishing their pockets before the next presidential election. They use every expedient to extort money from both shipmasters and seamen; and instead of facilitating commercial enterprises for their countrymen, they only place obstacles in the way.[10]

Captain Strickland paints a dark picture of the various parties in control of a sailor's life. They lie, cheat, extort, and torture. Strickland considers that "[t]he sailor is regarded simply as a machine to make money with, that needs no repairs; and so he is taxed to his utmost capacity of endurance."[11] The author reminds the public of the sailor's role in society.

It is astonishing how ignorant our national representatives are of the wants and necessities of seamen. Here are nearly a hundred thousand of the most deserving of our fellow-citizens, who, if they had families the same as other men, would represent half a million of our population; and not a single soul to plead their cause intelligently, or represent them in Congress. . . . These are the very men, too, who bring us all our necessaries and luxuries from foreign lands—the men, too, that choked the South to death in the secession war—the men, too, whose life-blood would be required, in case of a European war, to keep our enemies at bay.[12]

Before he appeals to others to help find a solution to bring the miserable sailor out of the depths, Strickland himself has one part of the answer: give him religion.

When I first took charge of a vessel, I felt my responsibility to seamen keenly. . . . It caused me so far to overcome my natural reserve and diffidence, that I immediately resolved to hold divine services every sabbath on board of any vessel that it might fall to my lot to command; and I have never yet seen occasion to regret my decision. The men would generally all attend and conduct themselves in a becoming manner. They would also behave much better during the voyage than if no such services had been held.[13]

Besides regular worship services, Strickland suggests another measure which should be put into practice to improve the sailor's lot: book libraries shipboard, such as those furnished by the Seamen's Friend Society that he was familiar with in Boston.

Strickland feels strongly about another means of influencing sailors to lead a righteous life: the captain's family.

> Another cause which operates favorably to dispose the minds and hearts of seamen to receive moral and religious truth is the presence of females and children on board of a ship. A great many shipmasters now carry their wives with them on some of their voyages; and those among them that happen to be devoted Christians can exert an influence for good among seamen that could hardly be exceeded by a minister of the gospel.[14]

Captain Strickland is very familiar with the financial means at the disposal of sailors. He takes the trouble to estimate in considerable detail the sailor's income and to calculate his expenses, concluding that what a skilled sailor earns is rarely enough to live on as a single person, much less support a family.

> Sailors, on an average, do not get work more than ten months in a year, and it is very doubtful if they much exceed nine. They have to go to boarding-homes at the close of every voyage, to await their pay-days, and look for other chances; and as voyages as now conducted, do not probably average in length over three months, it is easy to see where the time is consumed. Sailors probably average two or three weeks on shore. . . . Then they have to pay a dollar per day for their board while waiting, and eight or ten dollars, perhaps, in the course of a year to have their baggage transported; which, together, we will put down at the minimum sum of seventy dollars. They require more clothing than landsmen to keep them comfortable; and as it is sometimes scarcely possible to keep any thing dry for weeks, their garments rot quickly, which makes it necessary to buy more or less new articles every time they come on shore. Then, again, they

are charged enormous prices; and, as the fabric of which their clothing is composed must be woollen in order to keep them as much as possible from rheumatism, it necessarily costs very dear without extra extortion. If we put the sailor's bill for clothing at seventy-five or eighty dollars per annum in these times, it will be about as low a figure as he can possibly use and make himself decent and comfortable. Then again, he has to pay hospital money, which amounts to $4.80 per year; and frequently he has to fee shipping-agents for chances; and his traveling-expenses, bills for washing, and a dozen other little items, amount to something; so that, putting every thing together, his own personal expenses cannot possibly amount to less than a hundred and seventy-five dollars a year; and probably two hundred would come much nearer the truth. Now let us see what he gets. The highest wages now paid to seamen from the port of Boston are twenty-five dollars per month for short voyages, and eighteen or twenty for long ones. Assuming the former figures as the basis of our calculations, *and assuming, also that seamen are never shipwrecked, driven ashore in foreign ports, nor cheated in any way* [Strickland's italics], and we have the sum of two hundred and fifty dollars for ten months' work; but it is safe to say that sailors do not get as much as that one time in twenty. If, now, we subtract from this sum his necessary expenses, which we have reckoned at a hundred and seventy-five dollars, we shall have seventy-five dollars remaining, which [does] not pay the rent of two good rooms in the vicinity of such a place as Boston, and leaves no margin whatever which could be used for the support of a family. A common day-laborer along the wharves gets from thirty to fifty cents an hour; and, if he cannot get work over half the time, we see that his earnings amount to more than double the sailor's. A sailor's work, too, calls for skilled labor, and requires four years' service from a man of good abilities to master all of its mysteries.[15]

Strickland sees a direct relation between the impecuniousness of sailors and their remaining single throughout life. *"Sailors do not*

*marry, because their limited means will not allow them to support families,
or even to think of such a thing* [Strickland's italics]."[16] We shall see,
too, that the most of [seamen's] miseries and misfortunes are due to
the fact that they cannot have any homes of their own, because their
pay is not sufficient to enable them to maintain families.[17]

What is the solution? Strickland proposes that the national
government subsidize sailors in recognition of the services they
render the country.

> How can the nation change freights, break up bad seamen's
> boarding-houses, and give her sailors rights and wives and
> homes and property? Simply by adopting them as her wards,
> and giving them a small pension, which, with what they can
> earn at sea, will be sufficient to maintain their families in
> the most humble manner. Such a measure should have the
> effect to create, at least, fifty thousand new homes in the
> United States, and raise a hundred thousand people from
> almost the lowest depths of degradation and vice. It would
> give to the nation from seventy-five to a hundred thousand
> of the very best kind of seamen to man her navy in case of
> a foreign war, and also make it easy to carry out the law
> which requires that two-thirds of the crew of every vessel
> shall be American.[18]

Strickland has thought through carefully the details of a financial
package that one would tender to sailors.

> We will grant to every such seaman the sum of ten dollars
> per month, if he have only a wife, and two dollars extra
> for every child (not exceeding five) under ten years of
> age; and what the result be, allowing that fifty thousand
> heads of families had the full number to support we have
> just mentioned? Twelve millions of dollars. Allow another
> million to regulate the machinery of the movement, and we
> have thirteen millions, or a little less than thirty cents per
> head for the whole population of the United States.[19]

The author has also assembled other financial figures regarding what is at stake in the bigger picture.

> A man in charge of a vessel worth fifty thousand dollars, carrying a cargo valued at, perhaps, one or two hundred thousand, and several passengers, ought, at least, to receive as much compensation as a head clerk in a wholesale store, or the principal teacher in one of our common schools; but such is not generally the case. Shipmasters' wages are not fixed; but, as a general thing, they cannot earn over a thousand dollars a year in clear money.[20]

Appealing to the American public to see things the way he does, Strickland asks:

> We see before us a poor, houseless, homeless, wifeless, childless, joyless, suffering outcast from society, desiring to be fed with some of the crumbs which fall from our national table of Thanksgiving, and shall we spurn him away?[21]

At the end of the book, Strickland has composed an "Invocation," a 178-line poem of iambic tetrameter couplets arranged in quatrains. It is the only poetry he is known to have written (he writes "P. Strickland" at the end of the poem to allay any doubt of authorship). The poem includes numbers in the margin that refer the reader to numbered paragraphs of the book where similar thoughts have been expressed in prose.

Somewhat reminiscent of the tone and style of Alexander Pope or Samuel Butler, the poem is punctuated by invocations of God, Jesus, and celestial Wisdom. Strickland invokes "Great God," sympathizing with the plight of sailors as an example of fallen man in need of divine aid.

> Great God, we bring before thee now
> Those men that stormy seas do plough;
> And, oh! we pray our hearts may feel
> While they to us their woes reveal.

Strickland then proceeds to give a poetic inventory of these woes: "mighty tempests," shipwrecks, hard labor, pain, and poverty. Those classes of persons that exploit sailors are likened to sharks that "have gulped and swallowed all." The sailors have risked their lives and limbs to provide useful foreign goods to the wealthy. They should be rewarded for their "toiling hands and willing feet." With a final invocation to "Great God," Strickland suggests that nations, Christianity, and seamen should mutually serve each other.

It is hard to argue that Strickland, in any major way, misdiagnosed the sailor's condition. It is reasonable to posit that with an increased income stream, some sailors might use the windfall to found a family and mend their ways. Although the proposition that the U.S. government subsidize sailors appears improbable today, the American government has certainly subsidized farmers and means of transport such as railroads. Unfortunately, Strickland's voice from the deep was one of only a few that argued passionately in favor of the American merchant seamen and lamented their dismal condition.

Strickland's contemporaries who read the book would have gained a new understanding of the multiple ways in which common sailors were exploited, but would not agree that anything much could be done about it. They would have gained a new appreciation for the dangers sailors constantly faced in order to bring to America coveted items from abroad. However, they would be baffled as to how more change in a sailor's pocket would raise his standards, and certainly how those additional coins might get there.

Whatever its impact on public policy, the book gives us valuable insights on its author. Keen to improve the conditions he knew so well through his life at sea, Strickland put his thoughts in order and managed to convince a publishing house to communicate his ideas to a wider audience. Sea captains have often kept diaries and occasionally written memoirs. Much more rarely do we find one who so vigorously pleads a cause. As in his notes on slavery, Strickland not only observes a problem, he works out a solution.

4

Merchant in

West Africa

COMPAGNIE FRANÇAISE DE L'AFRIQUE OCCIDENTALE.

COMPTOIR DE *Rufisque*   *Rufisque, le 27. 7. 1901*

Télégraphe: SÉNAFRICA

COMPTABILITÉ.

Monsieur Strickland
Consul U.S.A.
Gorée

L egitimate American trade with Senegal began around 1800, when the British were in charge of the territory. "Legitimate" is the term used in contemporary scholarship to refer to trade not related to the transportation of slaves. New England sea captains in leaky wooden schooners less than one hundred feet long plied the Atlantic laden with tobacco, rum, lumber, beef, pork, flour, and other American products. Of all American products, tobacco was the most popular in Senegal. "Tobacco is money to the natives," wrote Samuel Swan (1779–1823) of Medford, Mass., master of the brig *Federal*, after a visit to Gorée Island in 1816.[1] Swan discovered that the tobacco leaf was highly valued and used as a ready means of exchange of goods.

By 1812, horses had been introduced on Gorée Island. U.S. exports to the island included saddles, bridles, whips, and spurs. On return voyages from Senegal, the American vessels carried as cargo animal hides, palm oil, and gum products. Gum was often used in the calico block printing process in the textile industry.

By 1822, the territory of Senegal belonged to the French again, and would remain so until independence in 1960. Captain George Howland (1797–1878) of Providence, Rhode Island, traveling on the brigantine *Argus*, found the market at Gorée glutted. From Africans he purchased zebus—cattle with a hump on their shoulders—for ten dollars a head. The French governor began to limit the products American traders were allowed to import into the colony. The French welcomed both tobacco and lumber for their own use, however. In 1829, Howland wrote about the restrictions and suggested the need for an American consul to facilitate trading in Senegal by American merchants. "Our government should look to this, and protect its commerce from such imposition from these colonial governments, and have a consul or commercial agent in all of them."[2]

Peter Strickland would become that consul over fifty years later, after the American trade with West Africa had already begun to decline. However, in his early years as a resident in West Africa—initially in Portuguese Guinea and then in Senegal—he devoted himself completely to trade. In about 1876, Captain Peter Strickland gave up command of sailing merchant vessels on the Atlantic to become a resident agent for commercial sales in West Africa. As early as 1861, the year of his marriage, he had thought about leaving the sea for something quite different. "I have been thinking seriously on the subject of quitting the sea for a business."[3] When he did leave the job of sea captain to enter the world of maritime business, he did not leave the sea. He built on the strength of one experience to launch into another.

The possible reason for the change was that Boston ship owner Matthew Bartlett, who had a high opinion of Strickland, made him a good offer. The captain may have seen it as a natural step in his career, making use of his maritime and business knowledge but from a fresh perspective. Bartlett had first asked Strickland to take such a resident position in 1864. At that time, Strickland was wary of living in Africa, considered the White Man's Grave. Now, over a decade later, despite the health risks, he agreed to live and work in West Africa. After a few years in his new position, however, in a letter written in Bissau, he summed up his African existence in these frustrated terms:

> I have a great work to do and it makes me almost faint to think of it. It is four hundred miles from one end of our accounts to the other: the way is beset with fevers, plagues, heats, rocks, sand-banks, calms, tornadoes, impecunious traders and mosquitoes: my only conveyance a little skip-jack of a vessel her cabin stifling with Bilge-water. I must make two voyages to the Rio Nunez, three to Cacheu, and I don't know how many to Gambia & Senegal, besides having all the care of the business on my mind at all times.[4]

Strickland was hardened to the dangers of the seafaring life—one fraught with danger, but one that he could dominate. He had become accustomed to the heat of tropical Africa, with its periodic epidemics of yellow fever and constant threat of malaria. Yet when he took on the management of business accounts spread along a four-hundred-mile coastline, he found himself overwhelmed. Strickland kept the books for all eighty accounts of the import-export trade he conducted for two Boston ship owners: Matthew Bartlett from 1876 to 1880 and, when Bartlett died in 1880 after closing down his business interests in West Africa, for Francis C. Butman from 1883 to 1884. From 1888 until 1905, Strickland would act in Senegal as an independent commission agent.

The large number of different accounts to maintain and the frustration of not being paid for merchandise made Strickland's job exasperating. Before going on leave, Strickland shared with his neighbor and business associate Claude Potin in 1903 a list of the only firms to which he could allow credit: Maurel & H. Prom; Maurel & Frères; L. E. Buhan père fils; Pascal, Buhan; A. Maurer; E. A. Offret; A. Teisseire; L. Assemat Frères; Devès & Chaumet; E. Chavanel; A. Delmas & Clastres; and Vézia & Cie. The list reveals that many Strickland customers were the big French trading houses with branch offices in the four major Senegalese ports of Gorée, Dakar, Rufisque, and St. Louis.[5]

Of these twelve French companies, the most well known was Maurel & H. Prom. Hilaire Maurel and Hubert Prom of Bordeaux founded their trading company in 1831 on Gorée. Maurel & Frères was created in 1869. The Maurel and Prom families left the Senegal trade only in 1928, after a remarkable century-long presence. At their height, they ran fifty factories in Senegal, where peanuts and gum were prepared for shipping to Bordeaux.

Maurel was so big in Gorée and in all of Senegal that the firm became Peter Strickland's closest business partner. Strickland sold American products to Maurel and bought African products from them. In 1905, when Strickland would finally close out his business connections and leave the consular service, he sold his import-export business to Maurel & Frères. Maurel also bought a piece of property Strickland owned in Dakar.

While Strickland had no pretension of rivaling the Maurel empire, he still needed to conduct his business affairs in an efficient manner. In a business relationship, information exchange has always been a crucial element. The meticulous Strickland was well aware of the methods to insure successful and rapid communication. First, he would number the letters he wrote to business associates. Numbering was a government requirement for writing consular dispatches, which he applied to his business life, such as his correspondence with his principal collaborator for many years, the Luckett-Wake Tobacco Company in Clarksville, Tennessee.

Second, he would set aside time in his schedule to cloister himself within his "writing cage," an iron structure with mesh sides, which covered his writing table and chair. There, unmolested by mosquitoes and flies, he prepared correspondence which would leave in the steamships that stopped in Dakar before continuing on to Europe. The mail boats regulated the colonial business world in coastal African towns, as a lifeline to one's metropolitan headquarters. One kept careful track of arrivals and departures of the regularly scheduled steamships called "packet" steamers. Strickland often wrote in his journal his expectations for receiving mail from various sources, which might be on such or such a steamer. He would express his disappointment when such mail did not arrive on time.

Third, Strickland developed a system to increase chances that his mail would be delivered. He used a postal scale to know the precise postage to affix. He knew all the sea captains on the Gorée-Boston run, many of whom would carry special messages, even packages, for him. He occasionally sent cables to business associates in the United States or France indicating the names of the vessels on which they could anticipate receiving mail he had sent.

Fourth, Strickland was keenly aware of the time delays in mail delivery that resulted when correspondents used different addresses. During the twenty-five years that Captain Strickland resided on Gorée, the official name for the island town was "Gorée-Dakar." In 1902, Strickland quantified precisely to Harpers in New York the loss in days. "The consulate is named Gorée-Dakar, but adding Dakar causes the loss of one day in transit, and to omit via France sometimes causes a loss of a week or ten days."[6] Over the years, the number of direct vessels from the United States to Africa diminished.

Each colonial power in Europe had its own steamship transportation system and schedule to its African possessions. In

1885, Strickland had already clarified to Harpers the difference in time delays when "via England" was penned on an envelope. "Probably the reason why some numbers of the "Weekly" do not reach me promptly is that they have "via England" on them for a direction instead of "via Bordeaux" which is the true direction. The English steamers are long in coming and very irregular as to time while the French steamers from Bordeaux are very fast and arrive here punctually on the 14th and 29th of each month."[7]

Strickland rarely used telegrams, considering them too expensive. However, when he was expecting merchandise—as opposed to routine mail—and it did not appear on schedule, he sent cables to his correspondents along the route. For instance, he sent a cable to a correspondent in the Canary Islands asking about a ship bearing his commodities. The correspondent cabled back that he had not sighted the vessel. The message served to alert Strickland to expect a delayed arrival of his merchandise.

Strickland's style as a business correspondent in French must have produced some smiles if not contempt. Never trained in the French language, Strickland nevertheless did not shrink from expressing himself in French in many business letters. In 1990, he began a letter from Gorée to a senior French official in the colony, "*je vous adresse en mauvaise francaise. . .* (I am writing you in bad French)"[8] In another letter he wrote "*Il a mouri*," where the grammatically correct phrase would be "*Il est mort*," meaning "He is dead."

Many of his French friends, business acquaintances, and official colleagues must have gotten a few laughs out of Strickland's attempts at French. Strickland himself was amused. In a self-assessment of his language proficiency, he wrote to French friends in St. Louis, "my French is not yet like that of the 'Academy.'"[9] One trick Strickland used was to list in a notebook the appropriate formulas in French with which to close letters. When needed, he could extract the most appropriate one for the occasion.

Despite his deficiencies with the language, Strickland did not appear to shy away from trying to use French when he had to. No American consular and diplomatic training program existed during the first several decades of United States history, and, later programs did not include language training until 1902.[10]

Aware of his own lack of training, Strickland was particularly proud of his son George's French language abilities. George learned the language by using it every day from a young age, while father Peter was about thirty years old before he heard much French. Evidence suggests that George tried to learn the major local language spoken in the colony of Senegal, Wolof (Jolof): among the Strickland papers in the Mystic Seaport Library is a *Grammar of Jolof Language*, with George's name written on the cover.

As a merchant in West Africa, Peter Strickland had to be a master of communication of some sort to survive, even though he never spoke in an African idiom, and barely in a colonial tongue. He had to deal with suppliers and buyers, with customs officials and government authorities, and with dockers and mariners.

What exactly did the United States send to Senegal in Strickland's day, in wooden sailing vessels one tenth the length of a modern-day container ship? The main export product was leaf tobacco, twenty-two to thirty inches long, grown in Kentucky and Tennessee. Transported in barrels, the tobacco traveled for ten days by the Chesapeake and Ohio Railway Company to reach the port of Boston. Traveling through eight States, the C & O Railroad was built in the 1860s and 1870s for the most part by freed black slaves, some of whom might conceivably have come from Senegal.

Peter Strickland dealt principally with one firm, the Luckett-Wake Tobacco Company of Clarksville, Tennessee. The Luckett Tobacco Company still exists today in Louisville, Kentucky. Luckett-Wake knew which farmers in the region sold the best tobacco. They learned how to best pack the leaf tobacco in barrels to protect it from becoming wet. The company was familiar with filling the orders it received from the Boston ship owners Matthew Bartlett and John F. Brooks.

Once, Strickland took his daughter to visit the Luckett-Wake Company, and once the owner F. D. Luckett himself traveled to Dorchester to meet with Strickland. Strickland dealt also with one secondary firm, W. T. Grant of Louisville, Kentucky. This was his backup alternative, when his arrangements with Luckett-Wake did not work out. Strickland kept in touch with the tobacco news in the southern United States by subscribing for thirty years to the Louisville *Courier-Journal*, a semi-weekly. After he left Africa for good, Strickland even contributed articles to the journal about the tobacco trade.

By far the greatest threat to the tobacco trade in West Africa that faced Strickland, Brooks, Luckett-Wake, and W. T. Grant was the development of a "tobacco trust" in the United States. The journal and letters preserved in the Peter Strickland collections over the period August 1903 through February 1912 offer several insights into the threat from the trust. In the first instance, Strickland writes from Gorée where he feels immediately threatened; in the last instance, he writes from Dorchester where he looks back at the experience from the vantage point of his retirement.

Strickland described the problem as originating in 1903, when the American Tobacco Company in the United States began to take over the business of buying tobacco from dealers in Senegal, with an aim to monopolizing the trade. They did this by buying tobacco stocks from dealers in Senegal at their customary price; first, they would sell low, and then when they had achieved a monopoly they would raise their prices. Thus, they gained complete control over the tobacco trade in Senegal. In addition, the trust would put any dealers—such as Strickland and his partners—out of business, if they did not "cooperate."

Strickland chronicles the takeover attempt, sometimes from month to month. In August 1903 Strickland learns for the first time that his trading partners have been invited to join the trust. They resist.[11] From Dorchester, where he is on leave, Strickland writes his clients in Bordeaux to share the news that he does not intend to enter the trust, and as a result may well have a large stock of tobacco, which he will not be able to sell. Further, he writes to W. T. Grant that he has seen Mr. Luckett. Strickland understands that both Grant and Luckett will continue to carry out their business notwithstanding the trust.[12]

Already by the middle of the following month of September, Strickland was receiving threats that if he would not enter the trust, the trust leaders would get all the African business without him. He wrote Luckett-Wake that he counted on his firm and W. T. Grant's company not to enter into any arrangement, which would leave him out.[13] Strickland was fighting for his business life, but was not becoming intimidated. On the same day as his letter to Luckett-Wake, he wrote his partner Macleod Reid in Liverpool, "Brooks read me letters in which Matthews says that the Trust will crush me if I do not go with them, but I have heard threats before and the principal effect they have upon me is to induce me to use measures for repelling the missiles."[14]

By the end of September, Strickland has learned that his French partners, the *Compagnie Française de l'Afrique Occidentale (CFAO)*, are now working for the trust.[15] Even Brooks has been "forced into the Trust, and is being employed by Matthews to try and coax me into it."[16] Strickland's partners Grant and Luckett still hold out. Strickland decides to explain to his neighbor and partner on Gorée, Claude Potin, the nature of the American trust and the danger it could cause. From Dorchester, he writes, "if they can manage to get everything into their hands it will I think be a very bad day for the merchant of Senegal, because a trust is like an octopus; it devours everything."[17]

The tobacco trust enjoyed relative success in Senegal by the end of 1903, as Strickland lost some of his best customers to it. He does not mention the trust for a few years, but by 1903 Strickland was seriously thinking about retiring from his consul's job and settling in Dorchester. He does just that in 1905, after having sold his tobacco concern to the French firm of Maurel & Frères.

From his retirement, Strickland closely follows the trust's progress and then demise. The trust adopts more violent tactics after its initial threats. Strickland writes to a colleague in Gorée in 1908, "On the night of the 3d of January however 100 night riders rode into Russelville where the Luckett-Wake Company have a factory and with dynamite and fire destroyed it, the loss being $15,000 or 75,000 fcs."[18]

Strickland feels vindicated when the American government tries to dissolve the trust. The trust appeals to the Supreme Court, which considers its methods to be unlawful. After a few years, the trust loses its appeal.[19] The war between the trust and the tobacco farmers is over. Strickland's last years in Senegal had to be among his least rewarding. He had realized that American shipping with the coast of West Africa had declined to a point of near disappearance. With threats from the trust and difficult relationships with his business partners, it is no surprise that Strickland thought more and more about leaving Africa.

Given the control that a colonial power exercises over a dominated territory, one may wonder how the United States enjoyed such a robust tobacco trade with Senegal at all. The World Exposition of 1900 in Paris allowed France to display its commodity strengths and to assess its weaknesses. That year, in an article entitled *"Le tabac dans les colonies,"* M. Laurent lists the world's leading producers of tobacco: the United States, Turkey, Brazil, the Dutch Indies, Cuba, and the Philippines; not France.[20] France consumed from forty-two to forty-eight million kilograms of tobacco each year. It produced only from twenty-five to thirty million. Algeria provided France with two to three million kilograms a year. Of the remaining fifteen million, the United States was the major supplier. The principal origin of American tobacco going to Senegal was Kentucky and Tennessee, and the major agent in the export trade was Peter Strickland.

The French diagnosed its own failings in the tobacco industry as poor production methods and the lack of outlets in France for the purchase and sale of the commodity. Admitting that tobacco production was relatively easy, the French regretted that they did not export any.

Tobacco was not the only commodity shipped from Boston to Gorée-Dakar over the period, but it was the most prevalent. To obtain an understanding of the full picture, let us examine one complete cargo list on Boston ship owner Francis C. Butman's bark, the *Jennie Cushman*. Between 1884 and 1891, this 274-ton vessel made twenty-two trips from Boston to Senegal and back. The July 1886 voyage carried an especially extensive list of different cargo items. The precise information was recorded in the consular forms, which Peter Strickland kept in his Gorée consulate. He recorded the measured quantity, the name of the item, and the stated value of merchandise that arrived on the bark *Jennie Cushman* from Boston at Gorée-Dakar on July 19, 1886.[21]

Table 3
Cargo from Boston to Gorée-Dakar on board Bark *Jennie Cushman*, July 19, 1886

QUANTITY	MEASURE	ITEM	VALUE $
202/2 Hhd	174955 lbs.	Tobacco	22068
400 Cases	4000 galls	Petrol	500
200 Bbls		Flour	1250
150/2 Bbls	15259 lbs.	Sugar	1070
15 Cases		Canned Goods	102
6 Kits		Mackerel	12
4 Boxes		Medicines	42
11 Cases	1100 lbs.	Paints	80
5 Cases	50 galls	Linseed Oil	30
5 Cases	50 galls	Spirits Turpentine	27
2 Cases	250 lbs.	Putty	12
20 Cases	200 galls	Tar	52
20 Cases	200 galls	Pitch	60
1 Crate	4	Sew machines	56
10 Boxes		Florida Water	35
25 Bales	1250 lbs.	Oakum	81
25 Kegs	2500 lbs.	Nails	75
1 Package		Table Cutlery	60
10 Kegs	200 galls	Hide Poison	210
1 Package		Brass padlocks	54
6 Nests		Tubs	15
12 Bolts	1208 yds.	Canvas	217
1 Bale	610 yds.	Canvas	85
33 Bales	29978 yds.	Domestics	2425
22 Cases	23089 yds.	Domestics	2088
72		Bedsteads	180
5 Bales	26	Mattresses	65
30		Tables	141
4		Wardrobes	57
18		Bureaus	175
5		Painted Chair Setts	113
12		Folding Cot Beds	16
12		Spring Beds	20
156		Chairs	250
10		Lumber	170
	26666 ft.	Lumber	442
6 Bales	600 lbs.	Tobacco	78

On form no. 120, Consul Strickland stated the total value of the cargo at $32,413. The first of thirty-eight items on the cargo list, 202 half hogsheads of tobacco weighing almost 175,000 lbs. constituted the principal transported commodity. The leaf tobacco packed in barrels accounted for 68 percent of the total cargo value.

The other American products consisted predominantly of manufactured wood supplies, foodstuffs, construction material, manmade cloth, and household goods. The reader will recall an earlier allusion to "hide poison." This product is directly related to the cargo that the ships would load for the return trip to the east coast of the United States. In order to survive the transatlantic voyage, animal hides and skins required treatment before being packed tightly into the hold. If the hides became wet, they would rot and decay. While the preventive treatment was not a substitute for curing or tanning the hides, it was thought necessary to protect them. Hide poison contained arsenic, applied to the hides while they dried in the sun. While the treatment would never meet today's environmental safety standards, in those days it was accepted common practice.

The *Jennie Cushman* loaded at Gorée-Dakar for a return trip to Boston, leaving Gorée-Dakar on Aug. 14, 1886. Table 4 shows the nature of its cargo.[22]

Table 4
Cargo from Gorée-Dakar to Boston on board Bark *Jennie Cushman*, Aug. 14, 1886

QUANTITY	MEASURE	ITEM	VALUE $
12053	51145 kilos	Hides	14626.24
1 Box	158 kilos	Hide Cuttings	17.5
22 Packages	2511 kilos	Rubber	1585.49
338		Goat skins	148

Strickland noted an "inward" cargo of thirty-eight items valued at $32,413 replaced in the same hold by an "outward" cargo of five items, valued at $16,377. Only two agricultural products constitute the entire load: animal hides and rubber. Over 90 percent of the valued cargo consists of the livestock products.

While the incoming and outgoing cargos on board the bark *Jennie Cushman* in 1886 represent one specific commercial exchange, many other types of commodities also changed hands. Strickland filled out another form no. 120, revealing dozens of other items of

American merchandise unloaded at Gorée-Dakar between 1884 and 1904.

Other principal articles of trade included: whale products, anchors and chains, cordage meat products (pork, beef, and ham), cattle, codfish and herring, lobster and oysters, oranges and apples, catsup, sarsaparilla, a sugar mill, a windmill, cigars and rum, baby carriages, bicycles, washstands and cradles, rocking chairs, organs and musical instruments, clocks and lamps, and ice. Most of these products would be sold to the large French mercantile houses headquartered in Bordeaux and Marseilles, which maintained branch commercial outlets or *comptoirs* along the West African coast. The outlets, in turn, would sell wholesale to French merchants.

Some readers will be surprised to learn that ice was transported from America to Africa. The French were eager to find ways to keep food fresh in the tropics. Natural ice was the only widespread means of refrigeration until mechanical refrigeration was developed in the early 1900s. How could natural ice survive a month's transatlantic crossing? Sometimes it didn't, as Strickland noted. Strickland's consular records show that over the twelve-year period 1890–1901, twelve ice cargos were unloaded at Gorée-Dakar. The largest quantity per cargo attained five hundred tons, transported in the three-masted schooner *José Oliviera* in April 1897. The cargo included three hundred bags of sawdust to help prolong its life. In 1901, the brig *Motley* brought only forty-two tons of ice. Afterwards, the item was dropped. Portland, Maine—especially the Kennebec River—was the source of the "harvested" ice.[23]

Similarly, the lone sample of African products carried on the *Jennie Cushman* did not reflect the entire range of Senegalese exports. Groundnuts or peanuts, and different types of fossil resins—gum arabic and gum copal—were among the most popular products exported to Europe and the United States.

Gum arabic from the acacia tree in Senegal was sought for use in the manufacture of confections, pharmaceuticals, inks, and adhesives. In particular, gum arabic was used to coat candies and pills, to treat silk and lace, to make ink and water-colored paints, and to provide stickum for envelopes. Gum copal was used to make varnish. Palm oil kernels used to make cooking oil also formed part of cargoes headed for American shores.

It is interesting to look at the block of twenty-one years by adding up the value column for each ship visit recorded. The stated value of inward cargo to the port of Gorée-Dakar over the years 1884–1904 was an average per vessel of $11,792, with a minimum of $40 for one cargo and a maximum of $53,343. The total value of inward cargo for the twenty-one-year period was $1,933,939. These data derive from records of 164 vessel stops.

The stated value of outward cargo from the port of Gorée-Dakar over the years 1884–1904 was an average of $8,461, with a minimum of $40 for one cargo and a maximum of $34,260 for another. The total value of outward cargo for the twenty-one-year period was $981,459. These data derived from records of only 116 vessel stops. Consul Strickland did not consistently record the value of inward and outward cargo shipments. Nevertheless, the data he did supply are significant, and convey a useful idea of the amount of cargo traffic in both directions. The value of American cargo going to West Africa ($1,933,939) was approximately double the value of African cargo returning to the United States ($981,459) over the period under consideration.

American vessels rarely went directly to Gorée-Dakar. Nine times out of ten on the way out or back they would make commercial stops in Cape Verde, Bathurst, Bissau, Sierra Leone, the Rivers of Guinea, and/or St. Louis or Rufisque in Senegal. The pattern of recorded stops was this: ninety-nine stops at a Cape Verde Island on the way to Gorée-Dakar; fifty-nine stops on the way home; fifteen stops at Bathurst inward bound; forty-nine outward bound; thirty stops at Bissau on the way to Senegal; twenty-eight stops on the way back; twenty-nine stops at other Senegalese ports coming in and twenty-six stops going out. Stops at Sierra Leone and the Rivers were rare.

Perhaps the most historically significant cargo Peter Strickland carried in his hold during his merchant career was cow hides from West Africa to make shoes for Civil War soldiers. When he brought peanuts from Senegal to the northern states, which had formerly bought that product from the American south, his ship owners made a handsome profit. Strickland wrote in 1864:

Dealers came down to see the hides today and I think a sale was effected at almost double the price which was paid for them in Africa. Our Soldiers are said to be very hard on shoe-leather, which contributes with other things to make the price of hides very high, and another article of produce from Africa, Peanuts, being cut off from our Southern States by the War are also very dear, so that Mr. Bartlett, the owner of the *Robert Wing* and of several other vessels in the African trade has every inducement to push the business for all it is worth. There is now talk in the office of buying two schooners for the trade on the Coast, and if one is bought under circumstances as they are at present I am almost sure of a chance to command one of them.[24]

Strickland's merchant career was long and rich, and documented in several forms: in his journal, his correspondence, his consular dispatches, and in the consular forms he was obliged to fill out when American vessels came to port in Dakar or Gorée. He is thus able to shed much light on the tobacco imports to West Africa from the southern United States, on the lumber and other imports to Senegal, as well as on the nature of exports from West Africa to the east coast of the United States.

During his twenty-one full years as consul, 1884–1904, Peter Strickland recorded information on 255 visits by American vessels. Many vessels made multiple voyages: the number of different vessels stopping at port was seventy-eight.

The vessels were composed of two-masted schooners (43), barks (13), brigs (11), three-masted schooners (6), and barkentines (5). They were built between 1858 and 1892 in shipyards located in Maine (45), Massachusetts (30), Connecticut (1), New Hampshire (1), and New York (1).[25] The range in tonnage was substantial: a high of 790, a low of 35, and an average of 304 tons. The high belonged to the bark *Willard Mudgett* of Boston and the low to the schooner *T.V.C. Hawes* from Chatham, Massachusetts.

One can divide the itineraries of the 255 visits into two equal categories: ships that moved up and down the west coast of Africa (117) and ships that made the crossing to and from West Africa from the east coast of the United States (115), plus a few anomalies

(3).[26] Data for the remaining twenty cases were missing from the consular forms. For most of the vessels coming from or going to the U.S., commercial stops were made on the way in West Africa, and sometimes (26 cases) in the West Indies or Venezuela.

Provenance included the following ports in 253 cases noted: Boston (92); Cape Verde Islands (76); Bissau, Portuguese Guinea (31); St. Louis, Senegal (29); Bathurst, The Gambia (15); Pascagoula, MI (3); New Bedford, MA (1); New York City (1); Newport, RI (1); Providence, RI (1); Satilla River, GA (1), Rio Nuñez, French Guinea (1); and Cardiff, Wales (1).

The destinations for the vessels after their stop in Senegal provide a different picture. Boston is no longer in first place. The itinerary includes some new ports. Of the 226 ports cited in Consul Strickland's reports, the breakdown is as follows: Cape Verde Islands (51); Bathurst, The Gambia (39); Boston (37); Bissau, Portuguese Guinea (28); St. Louis, Senegal (25); the U.S. in general (11); Barbados (9); Sierra Leone (6); Rufisque, Senegal (3); Providence, RI (2); Isle of May, Scotland (2); Apalachicola, FL (1); Casamance, Senegal (1); Orchila, Venezuela (1); Pensacola, FL (1); Turks Is. (2); Trinidad (2); Charleston, SC (1); Haiti (1); Fernandina, FL (1); West Indies (1); and St. Martin, Martinique (1). As the easternmost island in the Caribbean, Barbados was only seventeen days from Gorée. Vessels generally traveled in ballast to the West Indies, loaded sugar, and made the voyage to Boston.

The following table presents the class and name of the seventy-eight vessels, which stopped at the West African port of Gorée-Dakar at least once from 1884 to 1904, along with the name of their owner and homeport.[27] The vessels sailed out of six states, four of them in New England: Massachusetts (47), Maine (11), Rhode Island (8), and Connecticut (1). Of the 60 percent of vessels coming from Massachusetts, 53 percent belonged to the port of Boston. Ten vessels were from New York City and one from Philadelphia.

Table 5

Class, Name, Home Port, and Owner of the Seventy-Eight Sailing Vessels from the United States Stopping at Gorée-Dakar in Senegal, West Africa, 1884–1904

CLASS	NAME	HOME PORT	OWNER
		MASS.	
Schooner 3 Masts	*Albert L. Butler*	Boston	John S. Emery
Barkentine	*Annanwilde*	Boston	William H. Randall
Schooner	*Annie Fairfax*	Boston	Francis C. Butman
Barkentine	*Arlington*	Boston	Daniel S. Emery
Bark	*Auburndale*	Boston	John S. Emery
Barkentine	*Belmont*	Boston	John S. Emery
Bark	*Charles F. Ward*	Boston	John S. Emery
Bark	*Clotilde*	Boston	John S. Emery
Brig	*Edith*	Boston	John S. Emery
Schooner 3 Masts	*Elsie Fay*	Boston	W. H. Wilkenson
Schooner	*Fannie A. Spurling*	Boston	John A. Silva
Bark	*Hancock*	Boston	John S. Emery
Bark	*Hiram Emery*	Boston	John S. Emery
Schooner	*Jeanie Lippitt*	Boston	Peter H. Crowell
Bark	*Jennie Cushman*	Boston	Francis C. Butman
Bark	*John H. Pearson*	Boston	George H. Emery
Schooner 3 Masts	*Lamoine*	Boston	Daniel S. Emery
Schooner	*Lucy W. Snow*	Boston	Francis C. Butman
Schooner	*M. E. Higgins*	Boston	Francis C. Butman
Bark	*Megunticook*	Boston	Daniel S. Emery
Schooner	*Nantasket*	Boston	Daniel S. Emery
Brig	*Onolaska*	Boston	John S. Emery
Bark	*Rebecca Goddard*	Boston	Glidden & Bridge
Schooner	*Rebecca L. Evans*	Boston	Theophilus B. Baker
Schooner	*Ripple*	Boston	Francis C. Butman
Schooner	*St. Croix*	Boston	John S. Emery
Brig	*H. C. Sibley*	Boston	Matthew W. Bridge
Brig	*Sullivan*	Boston	Daniel S. Emery
Schooner	*Timothy Field*	Boston	John S. Emery
Bark	*Tremont*	Boston	John S. Emery
Schooner	*Wide Awake*	Boston	Thomas B. Lynch
Bark	*Willard Mudgett*	Boston	O. S. Glidden
Schooner	*T. V. C. Hawes*	Boston	A. G. Harding
Schooner	*William E. Terry*	Boston	Joseph O. Proctor
Schooner	*Clara L. Sparks*	New Bedford	Henry M. Brell
Schooner	*Freeman*	New Bedford	J. D. Hilliard
Schooner	*General Scott*	New Bedford	Mary L. Monteiro
Schooner	*Longwood*	New Bedford	Antonio H. Brito
Schooner	*Lula E. Wilbur*	New Bedford	Nathaniel P. Sowle
Schooner	*Oliver Cromwell*	New Bedford	Hendrick Morse
Schooner	*White Cap*	New Bedford	D. H. Rice
Schooner	*Hattie & Lottie*	New Bedford	José F. Machado
Schooner	*Alice*	Provincetown	J. H. Chase
Schooner	*Colorado*	Provincetown	Manuel Brazil
Brig	*David A. Small*	Provincetown	W. A. Atkins
Schooner	*Leon S. Swift*	Provincetown	Marshall L. Adams
Schooner	*Spring-Bird*	Provincetown	Frederick S. Doggett

CLASS	NAME	HOME PORT	OWNER
		MASS.	
Schooner	*Alice*	Provincetown	J. H. Chase
Schooner	*Colorado*	Provincetown	Manuel Brazil
Brig	*David A. Small*	Provincetown	W. A. Atkins
Schooner	*Leon S. Swift*	Provincetown	Marshall L. Adams
Schooner	*Spring-Bird*	Provincetown	Frederick S. Doggett
Schooner	*Charles H. Fabens*	Salem	C. E. & B. H. Fabens
		MAINE	
Schooner	*S. G. Haskell*	Deer Isle	E. A. Richardson
Barkentine	*Bruce Hawkins*	Machias	James Gurney
Schooner 3 Masts	*H. E. Thompson*	Machias	C. H. Thompson
Schooner	*H. E. Willard*	Portland	J. H. Hamlen
Brig	*Screamer*	Portland	W. S. Berry
Schooner 3 Masts	*José Oliveira*	Rockland	Seth C. Airey
Bark	*Beatrice Havener*	Searsport	T. W. Haven
Schooner	*James B. Jordan*	Thomaston	Charles H. Washburne
Schooner	*Levi S. Andrews*	Thomaston	Charles H. Washburne
Schooner	*Martha L. Thomas*	Thomaston	L. W. Watts
Schooner 3 Masts	*T. W. Dunn*	Thomaston	T. W. Dunn
		RHODE IS.	
Schooner	*Nellie May*	Newport	John Waters
Schooner	*David A. Story*	Providence	Luis d'Oliveira
Schooner	*John M. Ball*	Providence	N. W. Freeman
Schooner	*John Smith*	Providence	Oakes & Foster
Brig	*Motley*	Providence	Samuel L. Holway
Schooner	*Unique*	Providence	John F. Lewis
Schooner	*Willie G.*	Providence	L. Rogers
		NEW YORK	
Schooner	*Annie L. Palmer*	New York	W. H. Mitchell
Schooner	*Belle Bartlett*	New York	Allerton D. Hitch
Brig	*Daisy*	New York	John Swan
Schooner	*Herald of the Morning*	New York	Allerton D. Hitch
Barkentine	*John Swan*	New York	Swan & Son
Bark	*Justin H. Ingersoll*	New York	Swan & Son
Brig	*Kaluna*	New York	Archibald T. Henry
Schooner	*Lavinia F. Warren*	New York	Elijah A. Houghton
Brig	*Leonora*	New York	Leonora M. Blood
Schooner	*Mary A. Clark*	New York	George S. Cowl
		CONN.	
Schooner	*Ruth*	New London	R. R. Morgan
		PENN.	
Brig	*Charles A. Sparks*	Philadelphia	John C. Donar

Massachusetts accounts for 62 percent of the homeports, and of them 71 percent of the vessels are based in Boston. These figures demonstrate the predominance of Massachusetts in the West African trade. The single case of the schooner *Ruth* from New London is noteworthy as being the town where the consul was born and raised. The single-deck schooner *Ruth*, built in Noank in 1881, made a voyage to Senegal in 1902 with a cargo of cattle and fruit. The single case of Salem is interesting as Salem was the home port of most American vessels which traded with West Africa in the 1840s and 1850s.[28] The Emery family of Boston owned as many as eighteen of the thirty-four vessels from Boston. Many of his vessels were chartered by others—such as Matthew Bartlett's associate John F. Brooks—for African voyages.[29] The second Boston name of note is shipbroker Francis C. Butman: Strickland worked as Butman's agent in Senegal in 1883–1884.

In the first ten years, 176 American vessels stopped at Gorée-Dakar; in the last ten, only seventy-nine. Strickland noted the increased competition from the European powers and the decreased interest in the West African trade within the United States. As a New Englander, Strickland could be proud of the significant role his native region played in the African trade. The trade gave employment to ship builders and seamen; it introduced buyers in faraway Africa to a line of American goods. The longer Strickland stayed in Africa, however, the more distraught and disillusioned he became as he realized that America was losing out on what he considered a potentially huge commercial market. A sole American in West Africa playing roles of merchant, consul, and advocate was no match for the colonial organization of European empires, notably the French.

5

Resident on
Gorée Island

Department of State.

Washington, *February 2* 1895.

Peter Strickland Esquire,
   Consul of the United States,
      Gorée-Dakar, Africa.

A rare form of international recognition came to Gorée Island in 1978 when UNESCO named it among its twelve original World Heritage sites. The main reason for the island's inclusion was its importance from 1500 until 1850 as a depot from which Africans in bondage were packed onto slave ships and sent to the western hemisphere.

Gorée was on the world map as early as October 1664 for its role in a colonial power's historic decision. The history of Gorée shows five centuries of disputed ownership by Portuguese, Dutch, British, and French powers. From the Treaty of Vienna in 1815, Gorée became a French possession, until the independence of Senegal in 1960.

In August of 1664, the Dutch Admiral Michiel de Ruyter approached Gorée with twelve warships and wrested the island from British Governor George Abercrombie. On October 24, the English capitulated, with no blood: a show of force had sufficed.

The Dutch were then in a quandary. Spread thinly in both hemispheres as they tried to develop both the East and the West Indian trade, the Dutch determined that they should choose between two islands: Gorée in West Africa and New Amsterdam in the New World. Figuring that Gorée was of more strategic importance than New Amsterdam, the Dutch gave up the latter to a British fleet of warships without a shot fired; New Amsterdam, of course, soon became New York.[1]

Strickland's very first impressions of the island were quite negative.

I took a walk around Gorée for the first time, but found but little that was interesting. There were many naked children in its narrow streets, who however seemed to have some clothing on on account of their blackness, but apparently they had no notion that there was any impropriety in being seen naked. There are not many fine buildings in Goree, although the Palace where the Governor lives when he comes here is fine, the Church is a fairly handsome edifice and there are a few houses that look pretty well. Gorée was first built up because it afforded a safe place not far from the mainland for Europeans to live in and trade as much as they liked with the natives, who could molest neither them nor their property on the Island which is very easy of defense.[2]

Later, in addition to the positive features of trading opportunities and safety, Strickland would note the advantages of Gorée's ideally protected port, and a climate healthier than that of Dakar.

Neither Peter Strickland the businessman nor Peter Strickland the consul owned any property on the island of Gorée. His business and diplomatic sponsors did not believe in tying up scarce funds in real estate. Besides, the consular appointment did not come with a salary, only the authorization to conduct business.

In 1880, Strickland did not have to look far for a residence on the island; he moved into the quarters previously rented by Capt. Henry O. Skinner, his predecessor in Matthew Bartlett's import-export business. Skinner is known to have occupied the house in 1865; he died and was buried in Senegal in February 1879.

Strickland's correspondence and journal show that he rented from the same two landlords throughout his residency on the island, from 1880 until 1905. There were two rents to pay because Strickland rented two separate though adjacent houses.

The houses were located on the northern shore of Gorée overlooking the port. The large stone two-story structures were built by the French between 1820 and 1850 and included storehouse space for commercial purposes. Both Skinner and Strickland used the storehouses to keep leaf tobacco in barrels before sale. The storerooms were later removed. The houses are not known not to have been used for the slave trade; slave houses were located in other parts of the island.

Who were Strickland's landlords? They were both mulattoes, with French roots on the paternal side and Senegalese ancestry in the maternal line. The first landlord, Léopold Armand Angrand, was born in 1859 and died in 1906. A businessman on Gorée, Angrand served as deputy mayor for a time.

The second landlord, Xavier Boyer, was born in 1857 in Gorée and died in 1918 in Marseilles. His grandfather François Alphonse Boyer was born in the Var region of Provence and emigrated to Gorée. A businessman living in Dakar, Xavier had property and family on Gorée. The National Archives in Dakar list him as owning property on rue St. Joseph on Gorée in 1904.[3] Strickland's two landlords were related: Xavier Boyer's wife Ursule was Léopold Angrand's sister.

Strickland negotiated his own rental agreements, often drafting the leases himself. He paid 100 francs a month for most of the rental period. Sometimes he paid quarterly, sometimes semi-annually. Usually Strickland paid his landlords in cash. Once, however, he paid Boyer in kind, with tobacco.[4] In addition, Strickland rented a warehouse from Boyer for twenty-five francs a month.[5]

Peter Strickland hired a small staff of local residents to help him keep up the houses, clean the premises, cook and wash, and run errands to advance the tobacco sales business. A few lived on the premises; most did not. Two, Luis and Carlo da Silva, were holdovers from Strickland's years spent in Bissau. In various journal entries, Strickland gives some indication of names, jobs, pay scale, and character.

> Carlo da Silva, carpenter, handyman, storekeeper
>   100 francs/month. Sleeps on premises.
>   Tasks: shingle hen-coop containing Cape Verde Island hens; repair cistern-door; insert wire panels in Strickland's sleeping cage; paint Strickland's writing cage; make chests for the voyage to America; paint the safe; take tobacco samples to Rufisque; install locks and keys; build and install rain protector in front of verandah; make support for spy-glass; fix a steamer chair to use in making the voyage home.
> Charles Seck, handyman
>   Task: whitewash house.

Antoine Correa
    Task: repair the awning over the second floor.
Mowade, tobacco business helper
    50 francs/month. Sleeps on premises.
    Tasks: wash floors; fix up Strickland's Dakar lot;
    accompany Strickland to Dakar to be paid by creditors;
    accompany Mary Strickland to Dakar and back when
    she was invited to social events.
Luiz da Silva, cook
    30 francs/month. Sleeps on premises.
    Tasks: cook; feed the cat.
Madelaine, cook
Lydia, cook
    Tasks: make cakes and pies.
Marie Basse, maid
    30 francs/month.
    Tasks: clean office; wash up and air rooms; keep things
    about the house orderly and safe.
Marie Diouf (called Paule), maid
Lottie (Marie Diouf's daughter), maid helper
Marie-Therese Sagna, maid helper
    15 francs/month.
Marie N'Jean, "half domestic"
Marie-Anne Fall, domestic

In hearing about Strickland's staff today, Gorée residents have
commented, "Yes, those are still names we know on the island."
The employee whom Strickland writes about the most and whom
he appeared to depend on the most was Carlo da Silva. The national
census in 1904 classifies Carlo as a carpenter, states that he is a
bachelor (more on this ahead) and is illiterate.
    The case of Marie Diouf (Paule) was special. She worked a
long time for Strickland. "Poor Paul for whom I am repairing the
house has got the serious failing that she cannot seem to keep
from drink, but I have had her for help off and on for more than
20 years."[6] The master's devotion to his servant extended to her
family. As Strickland prepared for his departure from Senegal in
1905, he wanted to show his appreciation to Paule, who had cared

for his daughter Mary in a time of need. "Had 4 men employed carrying stones for the reparation of the House of Paul's mother. This promises to be rather an expensive operation; but I do not like the idea of leaving Paul in Goree without a place to shelter her from the weather when she was so assiduous in her attention to my daughter Mary at the time she had the Yellow fever and at all other times when occasion has required."[7]

From time to time, Strickland displays his contempt for local practices he observes among Senegalese. The perpetrators are often his own staff. After a reception he has hosted, Strickland faults his own staff for loss, breakage, and especially theft. He laments, "Spent the day principally in cleaning up after the feast of last evening. I found when I came to prepare for the dinner that a great many things had been lost, broken, or stolen, which obliged me to buy a great deal, and very much enhanced the cost of the dinner. The native domestics are mostly born thieves and with the most careful watching it is difficult to detect them in stealing, and yet they steal by the wholesale."[8]

Strickland notes that the domestic Marie N'Jean was pregnant in late August 1894. By January 1895 she had died. Her aunt requests a contribution from Strickland for the funeral expenses, which will include feeding the family of friends of the deceased who will gather to offer condolences. Strickland does not approve of the manner in which the death is celebrated. "Called on by Madeleine Gomez the aunt of Marie N'Jean who asked for sugar to help make a feast on account of Marie N'Jeans [sic] Death. I replied that I was willing to give necessaries to Marie N'Jeans children but nothing to assist in the Pagan observances of the natives."[9]

Strickland's notion of mourning did not coincide with local practices; neither did his idea of marriage and fidelity. Strickland was bothered by the fact that his handyman Carlo lived with a woman he was not married to. "Informed Carlo in the morning that if he would continue with me I expected him to marry the woman he is living with. This I know has disgusted him completely, because if he should do this there would be some difficulty about his getting rid of her whenever the caprice should suit him."[10]

Strickland found that his local hired help required constant supervision and prodding to keep at their work, and often lacked honesty. He lamented, "[a] discouraging thing about hiring the natives to do anything here is that when not looked after they in general immediately stop work. They want their pay however just the same when it comes night."[11]

Strickland's negative view of the African character remained consistent. In 1896, he wrote, "it is Characteristic of negroes always to want something from the tow-babs[12] in addition to what they have given them. It is very discouraging dealing with them because they so seldom show signs of real thankfulness when anything of importance out of pure generosity is done for them."[13]

To keep his valuables safe, Strickland maintained two safes in his home, one on the first floor, and one on the second. He needed to have currency for both domestic and business uses. Strickland once admitted, "Have lost the Keys of my safe, but think they have been stolen."[14]

Strickland would hire laborers to carry out specific maintenance chores on the house. He employed two masons to whitewash with lime both of his houses on all sides.[15] The Strickland house today sports colorful exterior paint in ochre and crimson; a century ago, it was all white.

A most important tool for Strickland was his postal scale, indicating how much postage he should affix on envelopes containing the many letters he mailed. He commended young Senegalese mechanics for their skill. "Got the blacksmith to mend my little 'Letter balance' which got broken by a fall nearly a year ago, and he did it so neatly and effectually that the balance is quite as good and looks almost as well as ever. Some of the Young mechanics in this country learn their trades very well."[16]

If Strickland found a mechanic he lauded, it was not the same for accountants. "At work on accounts which consume a large portion of my time and make me weary of writing. I am not able to get help in this country suited to my mind, and had rather go without than accept of the kind which . . . would make me almost as much work as they would save."[17]

Peter Strickland and particularly Mary Strickland liked to keep pets in the yard. They had cats and two monkeys—one called "Boogum"—in a monkey house. Passersby may have quickened their step when walking by the Strickland residence. Strickland wrote that he had to shift the "monkey-house to other side of yard to prevent the monkey from waylaying passers by in the brusque manner that he does now."[18] Mary had a rabbit that she kept in a birdcage. Peter kept in another cage his pet canary that he loved to converse with.

Peter Strickland's daughter Mary became an amateur photographer on Gorée, but none of her photos is known to have survived. In 1901, she corresponded with Eastman Kodak in America and ordered her camera, film, and darkroom equipment from the *Bon Marché* store in Paris. She used a darkroom in the Gorée home she shared with her father.

Mary Strickland asked her father for a piano. He bought one in 1896 from Colonel Maclean, the British consul in Dakar for 575 francs. He had a crate made and brought it over to their Gorée home on the ferry. In 1901, Strickland sold it for 600 francs. In 1904, when he visited Captain Cromie, the British consul, Strickland was astonished to find the same piano, which had made its way back to the British consul's house. Cromie had bought it back for 450 francs. While he had it, Strickland had a French military band conductor from St. Louis tune it. Strickland wrote the Baldwin Piano Company in Cincinnati, Ohio, in 1901, to try to get them to export pianos to Senegal. Strickland reported that a number of French merchants and military men had pianos in Dakar. Musical instruments were among American exports to Senegal during Strickland's day. Mary again persuaded her father to buy a piano in 1909, a few years after they settled in Dorchester, Massachusetts.

Outside, Strickland designed a flower garden, which he watered himself. His outdoor water cistern built to take in rainwater was an important adjunct to comfortable living. The roof was made of tile that required replacement before each rainy season. He fitted a canvas awning to the top of the house to keep out the dew. After a tornado blew it off, he replaced the awning with a tarpaulin. On the second-story balcony, Strickland erected a flagstaff, to raise the American flag on appropriate occasions. To watch out for American vessels, Strickland mounted a telescope and a spyglass on the southern side of his second floor. When he retired to Boston, he also arranged to have installed a looking glass on a supporting device to view ship activity in Dorchester Bay. Strickland frequently checked the temperature on Gorée, a factor that affected quality of life on land and on sea. He reported a low of sixty-one and a high of ninety-three degrees Fahrenheit in one season.

After renting and occupying the two adjacent houses for seventeen years, Strickland apparently decided in 1896 that he was putting too much of his business profits into rent. He notified his landlord Angrand that if he did not reduce the rent, he would move out. When Angrand did not agree to a reduction in rent, Strickland moved all his possessions as well as the consulate office next door to Boyer's house. For a year and a half, he made do with the smaller quarters. Then, Angrand agreed to the reduced rent, and Strickland moved back. He occupied both premises from 1897 until his departure in 1905.

Strickland noted quite carefully the different stages of his move from the Angrand to the Boyer house in 1896. In July, he covered the walk leading from Boyer's house to its kitchen. He estimated that he would need three hundred feet of lumber to do this. In November, he mounted pictures on the interior walls of the new consular office in the Boyer house and remodeled the archives. In December, he remodeled his office in the Boyer premises, moved his bed, and closed the door between the Angrand and Boyer houses by the kitchen.

While Strickland conscientiously worked to make his houses comfortable and to maintain them, his relations with both landlords were at times contentious. At one moment, he thought he might have to find other premises. There are three references in the Strickland papers over the period 1897–1902 to a possibility that government might transform the Angrand and Boyer houses into a hospital. Léopold Angrand wanted to respond favorably to an interest by the French administration in such a plan. He even approached Boyer to see if he, too, would cooperate.

> I understand that Angrand is very intent on making a good thing out of the Government, by letting his house for a number of years for the "Hospital Civil" and because he has been told that there are not rooms enough he proposed to induce Boyer to add the house that we now occupy, and to restore the connection between them. If he succeeds in this

it will of course be much against my interest, but I think the Government wants the Hospital at Dakar. . . . Most of the houses remaining at Goree are old, damp, and have about them much decaying wood, which cannot be very good for sick people.[19]

As a tenant, Strickland was helpless. He wrote, "I am threatened with being obliged to remove from the premises I have occupied now for more than 22 years. . . . the Government wishes to buy it with a view of converting it into a Civil Hospital. I have lived in the place so long that I almost forget sometimes that I do not own it."[20] The French must have looked at the premises and determined that their size would be inadequate. Strickland accurately foresaw the slow deterioration of Gorée and the robust development planned for Dakar, where the hospital was finally built.

Just as Strickland had some problems renting from Angrand, so did he with Boyer. Strickland had to remind him to replace the roof tiles before the rainy season. Strickland had some run-ins with Boyer in-laws on the island. He complained to Boyer, in his best French, that Boyer's sister's tenant made too much noise when he was trying to take a nap. Furthermore, their sheep made too much noise at night when he was trying to sleep. When Strickland talked to Boyer's sister about it, she responded with insolence. This is about as long a letter in French as one finds in Strickland's hand. It displays his poor command of French grammar, although he gets his point across.

> *Cher Monsieur,*
> *Je regrette à dire que la femme qui habite la maison de votre soeur, Madame Chambaud, n'est pas bonne voisine. Elle a le tapages la souvent, et souvent apres dejeuner il est impossible à avoir siesta pour les tapages. Pendant le moi d'avril elle a une mouton lié à la porte que criée toute de chaque nuit et quand je demandai elle à tuer la mouton ou lié dans une magasin elle repondu avec l'insolance. Quand votre femme etais la elle marche bien, mais apres votre femme etait parti elle ne regarder pas les autres. Je crois il serai bien si vous parlerez un mot à lui. Recevez Monsieur mes cordiales salutations,* P Strickland.

Dear Sir,

I regret to say that the woman who lives in your sister's house, Madam Chambaud, is not a good neighbor. She often makes noise, and because of the noise she makes after lunch I am not able to take a nap. During the month of April, she tied to her gate a sheep that bleated every night. When I asked her to kill her sheep or tie it up inside a warehouse, she responded with insolence. As long as your wife was there, she behaved. Since your wife left, however, the woman behaves with no regard for others. I think it would be a good idea for you to have a word with her. Cordially yours, P. Strickland.[21]

The 1904 Gorée census affirms that there were ninety-two Europeans domiciled on Gorée. More than any other, Strickland mentions the Potin family, his nearest neighbors. Right on the harbor, Strickland's house lay more in a commercial part of the island than a residential one. The Potins lived directly across from the consul, in a large stone house.

When Strickland settled in the Skinner house in 1880, he became close friends with four Potins, brothers and cousins: Claude, François, René, and Louis. They were all businessmen involved in import-export.

Claude Potin, in 1904, was the President of the Chamber of Commerce. In 1906, he was working for Maurel & Frères on Gorée. In 1916, Claude would become mayor of Gorée until 1917. When Strickland left Senegal in 1905, he left four boxes of books, stationary, consular forms, and other supplies—including his American flag—with Claude Potin, thinking a consular successor might be named rapidly and need the documents. (The next American consul did not arrive for ten years.) After Strickland left Senegal, he sent more than a dozen letters to Claude Potin, asking about news, giving news; sending photographs, asking for photographs. No papers appear to have survived from those that Strickland sent to Claude Potin. Potin would be the consul's last link with the part of Africa to which he had devoted most of his life.

François Potin had become an important contact for Strickland when they first worked as businessmen in Bissau in the 1870s. In 1903, when Strickland went on leave to America, he asked François to take over his import-export business for several months.

René Potin is another member of the Potin family who played a key role in Strickland's life on Gorée. In March 1888 Strickland proposed René's name to the State Department to be his vice-consul. This was only one month after Strickland's previous vice-consul, his own son George, had died. In May, the State Department sent a favorable reply to Strickland via the American legation in Paris. The appointment was not destined to last for long, however, due to some business intrigue.

In 1891, while René served as the American vice-consul, at the same time, he represented the American businessman Frank R. Butman. Frank R. was the son of Francis C. Butman, a commission agent at 34 Central St. in Boston for whom Strickland had worked. Son Frank considered Strickland a competitor, as by then Strickland had joined up as agent with the Luckett-Wake Tobacco Company of Kentucky. René resigned his vice-consular position upon pressure from Butman.

There was no sign of African participants in the social events Strickland describes on Gorée or in Dakar. The white contingent on Gorée belonged to a few professional categories: colonial administrators, medical personnel, clergy, the military, businessmen and women, and consuls. Strickland gives us few names. He was friends with Alexandre and Amélie Desproges who lived on rue de Dakar on the island. Born in Fort-de-France, Martinique, Desproges served as the postmaster of Gorée. "We shall have Dr and Madame Dumas and Lieutenant Manuel of the Castel at dinner with us tonight. There are not many just now in either Dakar or Gorée who go to see each other."[22]

Over the period 1880–1905, Dakar increasingly became a more important military, administrative, business, and social center. The population in Dakar increased from 4,000 to 25,000 over the twenty-five-year span. Of the 25,000, 1,500 were Europeans. In 1885, Gorée boasted not only the governor-general's palace, but also the city hall and the hall of justice. All consuls but the British initially established their consulates on Gorée. Then, one by one, they moved to Dakar. Dakar officials occasionally attended events on Gorée; those living on Gorée certainly often went to Dakar to participate in social activities there.

A year before Strickland left Senegal, he took his daughter for a round of calls in Dakar. Subsequently he commented that Dakar was overtaking Gorée, judging from the number of French wives who had accompanied their husbands assigned to Senegal. "In the afternoon, Sika and myself went to Dakar, and made calls on Madame Ficatier, Madame de Beaufond, Madame [George] Patterson, and Mr and Madame Portiere [director of the coal company]. We had on the whole a good day for it, and the calls were all pleasant. There are a large number of white ladies in the Colony now, enough to afford quite a Society, and in Gorée there were never so many ladies. The Yellow-fever Scare of 1900 is quite over, and has not set the Colony back ten years as was predicted of it."[23]

Strickland also adopted the custom of making evening calls on French neighbors. Accompanied by his daughter, he visited the governor-general's family and Strickland's landlord, among others. "Called with Sika on Madame Roume, the Le Begnes, and the Angrands in the evening."[24] Some of the visits were returned. "We were called on last evening by the wife of the Governor General, Madame Roume, who staid with us an hour."[25] When Madame Roume once sent some vegetables over to the Stricklands' house as a gift, the consul noted it with appreciation.

Proximity facilitated Strickland's friendly relations with French officials. The governor-general's palace stood a mere hundred yards from the consul's house, on the northwestern side of Gorée. After one courtesy call, Strickland did not report on their conversation, merely that the governor-general had kept him waiting. Consul Peter Strickland was invited to many receptions held in honor of visiting dignitaries, social occasions, and dances (Strickland admitted in his journal that he had never danced in his life). In addition to describing social functions he attended, Strickland from time to time would comment on the French administration and officials on the island.

One of the most symbolically significant visits during Strickland's stay was the 1904 visit to Gorée by Sir George Clinton, British governor in Bathurst, the capital of the British colony of The Gambia. Ernest Roume, the French governor-general of French

West Africa, had invited Clinton to stop at Gorée for a day's visit on his return voyage to London. The visit took place only a few months after the signing of the *Entente Cordiale* between Britain and France, marking a new era of cooperation after centuries of rivalry between the two powers.

As a local diplomatic representative, Peter Strickland attended the official reception for Clinton, whose visit merited a half page in Strickland's journal. He also raised the American flag over his consulate as a sign of respect.

> June 27, 1904.
> Ther 75 fahr: 24 Cent. Nearly calm in the morning, but a brisk breeze sprang up from N.W. later in the day. The British & African Steamer *Dahomey* arrived from Bathurst today with Sir George Clinton, the Governor of Gambia on board. He was received by the Governor General with a salute of 17 guns and entertained at lunch and at dinner at night. The band was got over from Dakar and played "God Save the King" and there were fireworks in the evening in his honor. The British Consul and his wife, Mr Mackie the Vice Consul, the Doctor of Bathurst, and a Mr Archer all came to our house to dress and we entertained them as well as we could. They all had to wear the clothing which formality has prescribed which is exceedingly uncomfortable in such warm weather. The *Dahomey* sailed about 11 oclock P.M.[26]

The Dakar-based French photographer Edouard Fortier photographed Clinton's visit to Gorée. The photo subsequently became a picture postcard, reproduced on page 108. It is a quintessential "colonial" card, depicting the pomp and ceremony of not one but two colonial powers, as administrators and soldiers stand in formations next to buildings that represent administrative and commercial control.

On the far right of the photo appears the American consul's residence and office building, with an American flag flying (difficult to make out in a reproduction, but quite clear in the original postcard). Strickland may be grouped with other dignitaries on top of the *batterie*, the platform with cannons behind the flags. The governors are passing in front of the honor guard. The French are wearing dress white; the Brits, their dress black. French soldiers are on both sides with Senegalese soldiers in the middle. On the left side, a musician is holding his horn. Other musicians stand to the right side. The uniforms and pomp, the brass band, and the fireworks lighting up the sky all make a dramatic showing of colonial rule.

The governor-general occasionally entertained his Gorée social circle outside of diplomatic functions. Strickland recorded an evening featuring a magician, followed by dancing.[27]

Whenever the governor-general left the island or returned to it, Strickland was expected to be among the officials present. Once when the dignitary left for France on the steamer *Magellan*, the government's weekly official paper the *Journal Officiel* noted Strickland's presence at the Gorée pier.[28]

Strickland did not approve of the governor-general's condescending attitude toward others, as exemplified by an incident at the Gorée pier: "Today the Steamer of the Governor general took the place of the regular Steamer at the wharf before it was time for the latter to start, thus demonstrating that in the republic of France the convenience of a high functionary must be considered before the convenience of the public. This however in the present instance may be more apparent than real, and it may be that the Governor-general, when he sees what is going on, will not allow of discriminations in his favor."[29] Even a few years later in his New England retirement, Strickland had not forgotten what he considered the governor-general's haughty ways. He wrote to his former neighbor on Gorée, Claude Potin, "Roume and his czar-like attitude offended a great manner of people."[30]

The American consul was not the only consul on Gorée in 1904: the Portuguese consul also lived on the island. In contrast, the British, Spanish, and Uruguayan consuls were stationed in Dakar, and the German, Italian and Belgian consuls in Rufisque.[31] The Italian consul Jean Guiraud had resided on Gorée until 1894, when he moved his operation to Rufisque.[32] The consuls were located according to perceived need and convenience. Curiously, Strickland never mentions his interactions with other consuls on Gorée. One could assume that their paths crossed constantly, on the ferryboat and at official events, but that in both consular and business matters they pursued distinct paths.

In the years that Peter Strickland lived in Africa, from 1875 to 1905, he attended some Sunday services but less regularly than in the States. The two colonies in which he resided, Bissau and Senegal, belonged to two predominantly Catholic countries, Portugal and France. Protestant churches were rare. In Bissau, he taught his female servants some English through Sunday school lessons.

On Gorée, he attended Catholic mass, although he did not wholeheartedly embrace the experience. "Attended at Grande Messe in the morning. I being a Protestant, am not much entertained going to these services, but I do not wish for the ignorant Catholics about me to think that I wholly discredit the religion which they profess, as indeed I do not. I do not think the Roman Catholic Life-Boat is quite as good as some others for permanently saving Souls, but so long as it has a capacity to save them, and is often honestly used for that purpose, it would doubtless be wrong to wholly condemn it."[33]

Accustomed to seeing in the United States a large church congregation at Easter, Strickland was astonished to find only a small group of worshipers on Gorée. "Attended 'Grande Messe' in the morning and was surprised to find that out of the European population of probably over a hundred in Gorée there were not a dozen at church although it is Easter Sunday."[34]

A year later, in April 1905, Strickland noticed that he had only his neighbor for company in hoisting a flag at half-mast in honor of Good Friday. Strickland pointed out that the reason may have been the conflict between church and state in France. "This being 'Good Friday' we put the flag at half-mast, and seemingly we had only Claude Potin to keep us Company. The government being at war with the Church, Government Officials do not now frequent the Church much, but I see no reason for not respecting Good Friday with its associations because of the hostility between Church and State."[35]

Brought up to expect a strict separation of church and state, from his retirement in Massachusetts, Strickland queried Potin on the outcome of the conflict. "You do not write how the Church is getting along in Senegal, but as the Pope has forbidden the priests to accept the conditions offered by the French Government I presume the Church in Goree must be closed. The Catholics here in Boston are very angry at the action of the French Government in interfering with the Churches and they have held several indignation meetings where eloquent speakers have expressed most decided opinions on the subject."[36]

During Strickland's time of residence, Gorée was more important than Dakar as a port for merchant marine sailing vessels. If a vessel with cargo for Strickland landed in Dakar, he used flat-bottomed barges to transport it to Gorée.

Gorée was certainly a less expensive place to live and work than Dakar. This was an important consideration for a consul who had to pay for his own lodging. Strickland figured that the rent in Gorée was about half that in Dakar. In Gorée, his tobacco and animal skins could be stored very near the port, whereas in Dakar the distances were longer. "Goree is much run down as a place of business but rents are far cheaper here than they would be on the main land and the proximity of the sea assists powerfully in keeping up the weight of tobacco stored."[37]

Strickland must have been among the best-informed inhabitants on Gorée. He regularly subscribed to four newspapers from three continents: the French *Journal Officiel* printed in Dakar; *The Day* of New London, Connecticut; the Louisville *Courier-Journal* from Kentucky; and the European edition of the *New-York Herald* from Paris.

He sent in a regular subscription check to Harpers for *Harpers Weekly*, *Harpers Bazar*, and the *North American Review*. He also remained an avid reader of books, such as Macaulay's *History of England* and Walter Scott's *Waverly* novels.

At New Year's, Strickland mailed out cards to his friends and acquaintances. In 1905, his last year on Gorée, he sent 150 of them, recognizing that it was not an American custom but that it saved him "a great deal of time and trouble." Expecting that the Smithsonian Institution would be interested in photographs from Senegal, in 1904, he sent four picture postcards to the Institution. (A century later, the Smithsonian had no record of them.)

From time to time in his correspondence and journal, Strickland comments on the way that Gorée has evolved during the quarter of a century that he spent on the island. We have very few other reminiscences on Gorée, making such observations all the more valuable. How else would we learn about the island characters— such as old port captain Texier, fruit peddler Marcel, and ice woman Pahn—that Strickland describes so vividly to us?

> Gorée, now that it has received such an accession to its population from the Military, is certainly not quite so dull a place as it was while you were here, and Madame Pahn is I think more contented with the quality of her business than she was then. "Marcel" still sells his rotten apples *"avec plaisir Madame,"* and old Captain Texier, now he has got a pretty daughter to escort to and from the Croquet grounds is rather more aimable than he formerly was.[38]

Since nothing grew on the island, local merchants had to transport all food from the mainland. Marcel's apples, although perhaps seldom fresh, would have been an imported luxury, not a fruit grown in Senegal. Texier was the captain of the port of Gorée.

Although Strickland lived for a quarter of a century on Gorée, there is scant evidence that he spent much time exploring the island. His various activities centered around his home with the occasional social outing or promenade on the wharf. Only once does he mention a walk to the other side of the island, eight hundred yards away. "Called on today by the Metins in the evening, when we made an excursion together to the extreme end of the island. At the South end of the island among the rocks we came across an immense number of pigs, which rather intimidated the women of the party from going further. Goree is at present, excepting the front part of it, in a very sad dilapidated condition and if things continue on the way they are now a large part will soon be in ruins."[39]

Strickland gives us rare insights into the early ferry voyages between Dakar and Gorée. The first two steam ferries put into service between the island and the mainland were the *Lily* and the *Saphir*. He noted in his journal, "The steamer *Lily* which has been plying between Goree and Dakar has been hauled out on the beach for thorough repairs. Her boiler was exploded some time since and it is probable that she must have a new one. The other Steamer, the *Saphir*, was taken off yesterday at noon, and did not resume her trips until noon today, so that we were without steam-service for 24 hours."[40]

By 1904, the *Moustique* and the *Nantais* had already replaced the *Saphir* and the *Lily*. The trial run for the *Moustique* was Jan. 3, 1904, with its inaugural voyage on Jan. 5. Strickland called the ride comfortable and rapid, but regretted the small size of the craft. While the first steam ferries carried up to fifteen passengers in the front and fifteen in the back, the second generation could hold up to a total of forty. The ferry schedule included more frequent voyages, as Strickland noted. "Gorée has declined much in importance since you were here, but it is now connected with Dakar by a good Steamer which makes about 8 trips each way per day, and so it is very easy to get away from it when one chooses. The steamer is all the time well-patronized and frequently comes as many as 40 passengers on a trip."[41]

Strickland reported on the second-generation ferries while admitting that he and his daughter did not use them very much. "The Old Supply-Boat the *Nantes* is now at work, the *Moustique* being hauled off for a renovation. The *Nantes* is not so comfortable nor as fast as the *Moustique*."[42]

Peter Strickland never lived in Dakar, but he did buy, own, and sell a piece of property in Dakar, 1,150 square meters of land in what was then the center of town, at the corner of the rue René Caillé and avenue Pinet-Laprade, between the railroad station, the post office, and the market. The lot had a wooden house with a water cistern on it, and was surrounded by a brick wall. Sometimes, when Mary Strickland was invited to a social event in Dakar, she would sleep in the house rather than return on a late ferry. The consul would send his houseboy to clean the lot from time to time.

Strickland had intended to develop the land so that his son George would be able to take over his import-export business. All these plans crumbled when George Strickland drowned off Dakar's Cape Verde peninsula in 1888. Strickland looked around for a buyer as early as 1890. In 1901, he was asking 25,000 francs for the property. Finally, in 1905, he sold it to Maurel & Frères for the satisfactory sum of 39,000 francs.

As Strickland prepared to leave the island for good, he cleaned up an old boutique he had used to sell imported goods. Through the sale of some leftover items, Strickland hoped to earn enough to finance the passage home for him and his daughter.[43]

One of Strickland's last visitors on Gorée was the census taker, who counted him among the island's population of 1,560 inhabitants. Of this total, 1,312 were indigenous, 156 were mixed race, and 92 were of European stock.[44]

10. In only one of the fifty volumes Capt. Peter Strickland left behind did he draw sailing vessels in the margins. This drawing is from an abstract log he kept while on a voyage to Senegal in January 1866.

11. During one of his early voyages to Senegal in 1866, Strickland filled in the bottom part of one of his abstract ship log pages with this drawing of a half brig displaying an American flag being towed near land by another vessel bearing what appears to be a French flag.

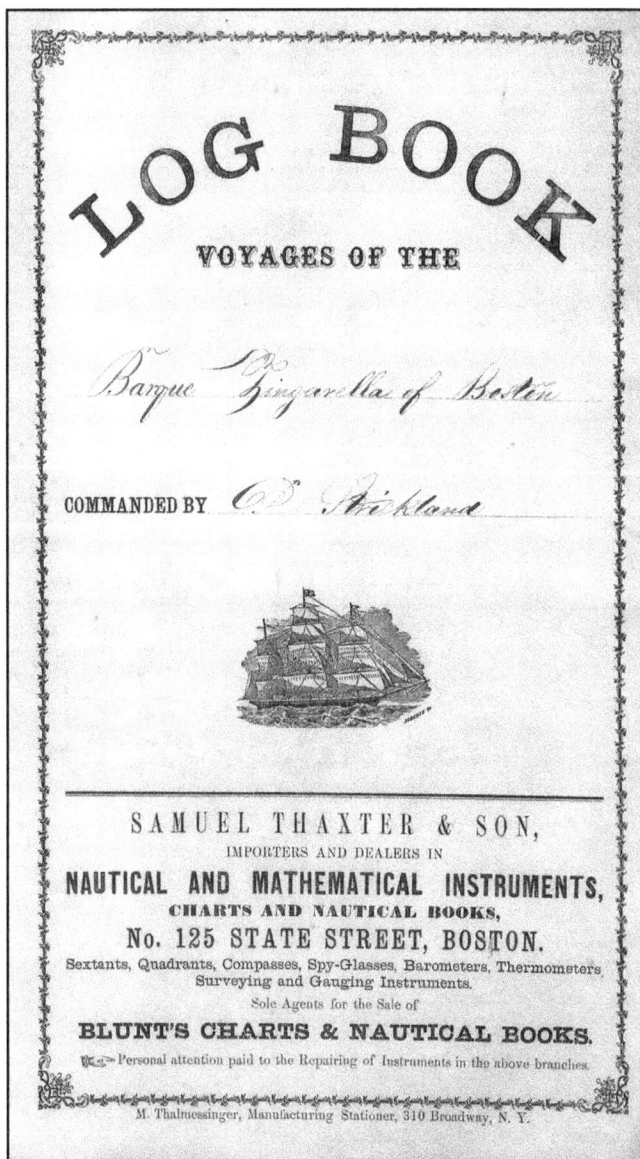

LOG BOOK

VOYAGES OF THE

Barque Zingarella of Boston

COMMANDED BY *C. Strickland*

SAMUEL THAXTER & SON,

IMPORTERS AND DEALERS IN

NAUTICAL AND MATHEMATICAL INSTRUMENTS,

CHARTS AND NAUTICAL BOOKS,

No. 125 STATE STREET, BOSTON.

Sextants, Quadrants, Compasses, Spy-Glasses, Barometers, Thermometers, Surveying and Gauging Instruments.

Sole Agents for the Sale of

BLUNT'S CHARTS & NAUTICAL BOOKS.

Personal attention paid to the Repairing of Instruments in the above branches.

M. Thalmessinger, Manufacturing Stationer, 310 Broadway, N. Y.

12. Between 1869 and 1882, Strickland transported American tobacco to West Africa in the 119-foot *Zingarella* and returned with cargoes of animal hides and gum from Senegal for delivery to ship owner Matthew Bartlett in Boston.

A

VOICE FROM THE DEEP.

BY

CAPT. P. STRICKLAND.

BOSTON:
A. WILLIAMS & COMPANY.
1873.

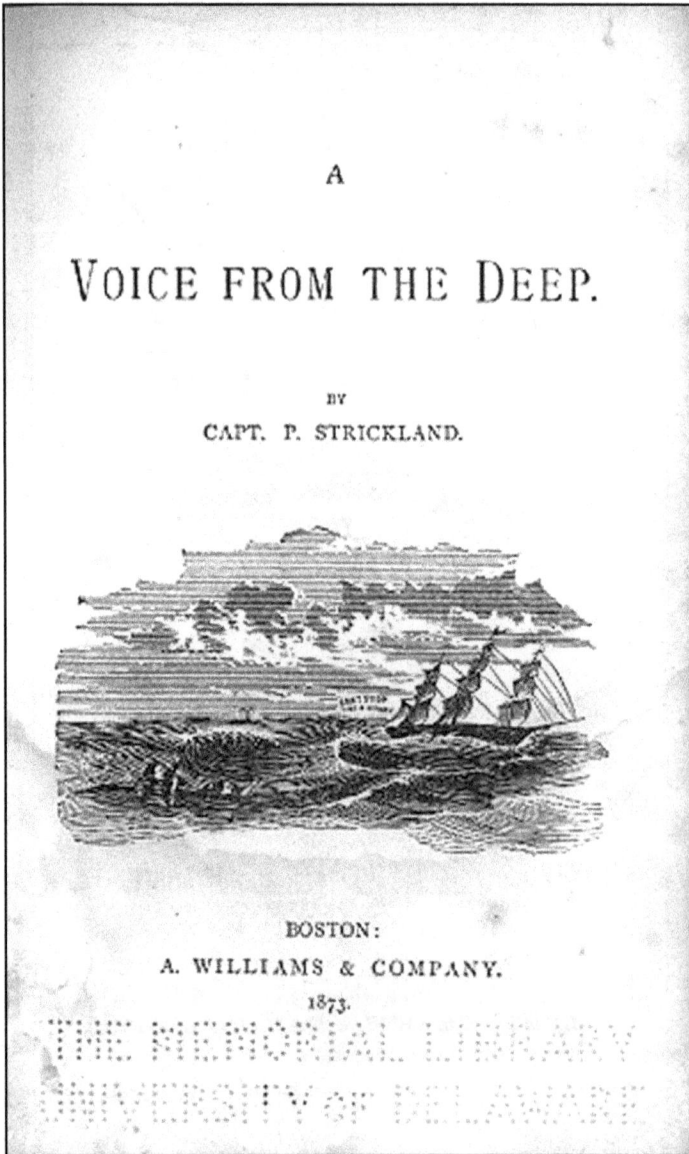

13. Captain Strickland found the time on board his merchant vessels to write a book on behalf of sailors. This cartoon on the title page depicts a three-masted schooner bypassing two overboard sailors and calling out, "Can't Stop, Time is Money." The book recounts the poverty and misery of exploited sailors and argues for a federal subsidy.

14. In 1905, Strickland sent a postcard of the port area on Gorée Island, Senegal to the Department of State. On it, he drew a large American flag over the consulate he occupied and a much smaller flag over the nearby home of the French president of the Chamber of Commerce.

SENEGAL – GORÉE – Réception du Gouverneur Anglais de la Gambie par le Gouverneur Général de l'Afrique Occidentale Française

15.   Thanks to the Strickland journal, the date of this photograph by Edouard Fortier was established. On June 27, 1904, the governor-general of French West Africa, Ernest Roume, received a visit to Gorée by the British governor of The Gambia, Sir George Clinton. The American flag is flying over the consulate on the far right.

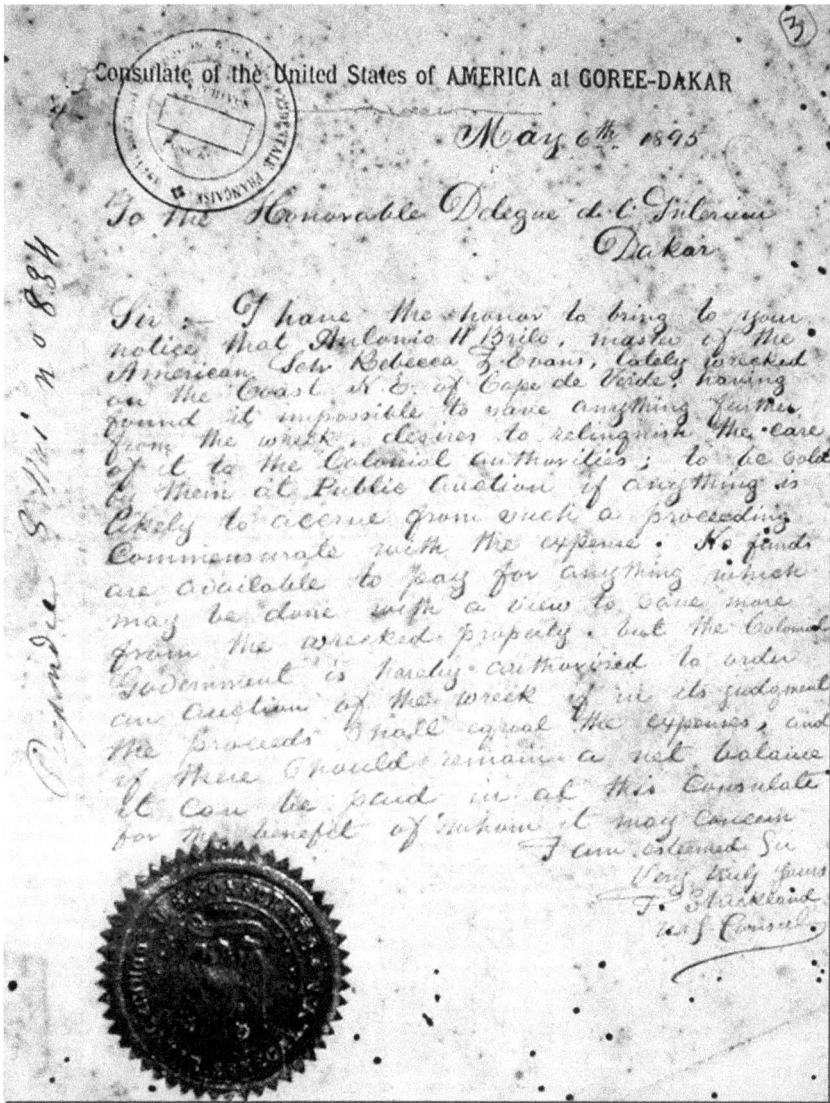

16. Writing in English in 1895, Strickland is inviting the French administration to organize an auction of whatever might still be salvageable from
the wreck of an American schooner off the coast of Senegal and turn over
any profits to the American consulate. The consular seal is a royal blue.

Consulate
of the
United States of America
Gorée Dakar April 18th 1904

Sir:— I have the honor to inform you that with the consent of your Government I am requested by the Government of the United States of America to perform Consular Services for the Republic of Panama in the French Colonies of West Africa until the Government of that Country Shall appoint Consuls of its own in foreign countries

I am esteemed Sir

To his Excellency. E. Roume
Le Gouverneur General de l'Afrique   Very truly yours
Occidentale Française   Peter Strickland
Commandeur de La Legion d'Honneur   U. S. Consul
Gorée

17. Strickland wrote to the governor-general of French West Africa asking for his consent that the American consul in Senegal represent Panama. Senegal gave its approval. The hand of American colonialism in Central America was reaching out as far away as West Africa.

18.   "Peter Strickland born in Montville, Ct. Aug. 1, 1837, died in Boston
Mass. Nov. 13, 1921. He was connected with Africa as shipmaster, merchant
and consul for more than 40 years serving as US consul for French West
Africa for twenty three years. Mary Louise Rogers his wife born in New
London Ct. July 29, 1832 died in Boston, Mass. April 19, 1915."

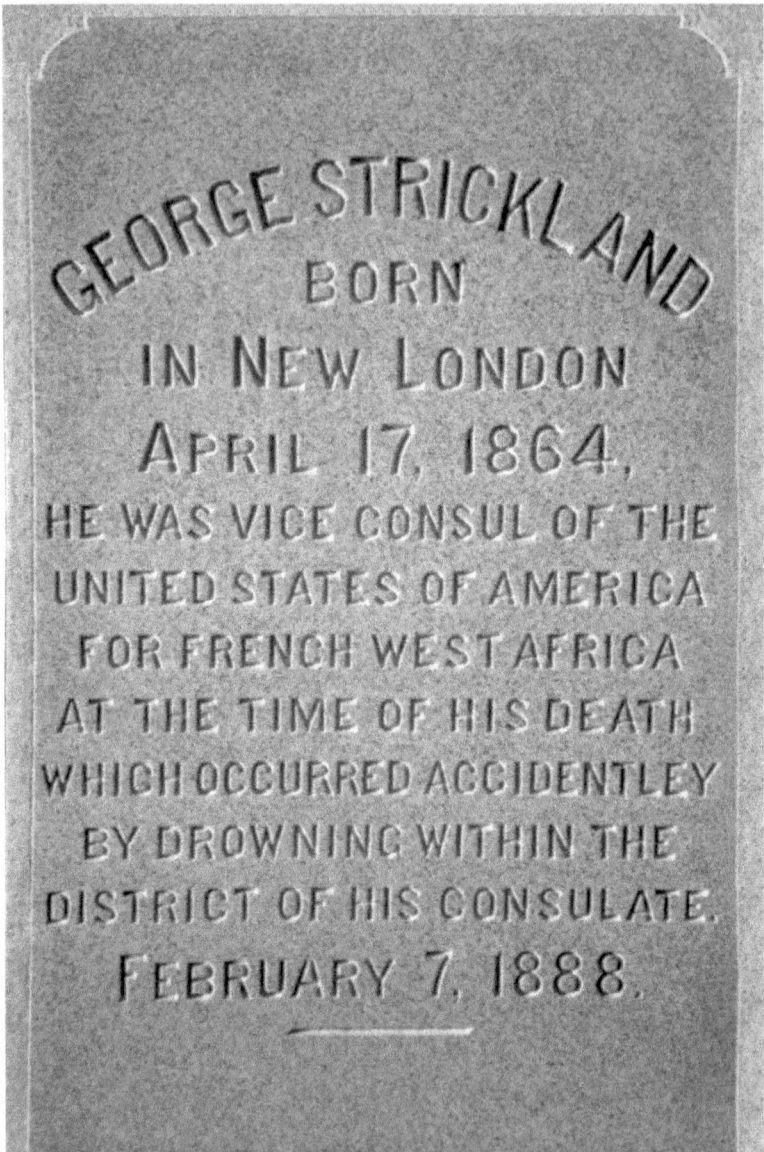

19.   "George Strickland born in New London April 17, 1864, He was vice consul of the United States of America for French West Africa at the time of his death which occurred accidentally by drowning within the district of his consulate. February 7, 1888."

6

Consul to Senegal

Your Obedient Servant
Peter Strickland
United States Consul for Senegal

The fledgling United States, through its Second Continental Congress, named its first consul (to France) in 1780. Unfortunately, he drowned on his voyage to Paris.[1] For its first century, America was represented abroad more widely by its consuls than by its diplomats. Diplomats were assigned mainly to European capital cities, while consuls sprang up all over the world in major ports reached by American shipping. Consuls tended to understand their countries better than did diplomats. American businessmen interested in foreign investment looked to consuls for the most useful information on trade issues.

One shortcoming of the consular corps was its wide door of entry. The basic requirements were simple: a male American citizen and not a felon.[2] Appointments were made through partisan patronage, and often resulted in ineptitude and corruption. The first serious inspection tour of U.S. consulates around the world, in 1870, revealed many serious failings.

Early consuls included authors James Fenimore Cooper, Nathanial Hawthorne, William Dean Howells, and Bret Harte.[3] During President Grant's administration, several Civil War generals and colonels who had served the North or the South were named. In almost every case, the applicant himself sought after the job, bringing to bear Congressional advocates or endorsements by other political friends of the administration.

By the time that Peter Strickland was named "Consul of the United States" to Gorée-Dakar, Senegal in 1883, the consular corps had amassed a century of experience and had already developed 161 forms to structure its profession and record its activity. Capt. Peter Strickland did not seek the job. The State Department went after him, which was unusual. Strickland revealed his attitude toward the consular job in a dispatch to the State Department in 1885. "My position with regard to the Consulate is this: as it came without seeking on my part so I am prepared to part with it as lightly if it so shall seem expedient for the Government."[4] If Strickland's tone appears a little huffy, it was because the American legation in Paris had refused his request for leave. He had the refusal overturned by explaining the situation to the Department of State in Washington.

Strickland was not the first U.S. consul in Africa. The United States had opened a consulate in Cape Town, South Africa in 1799, and on the island of Zanzibar in 1836. In West Africa, American consuls were assigned to the Cape Verdean island of Santiago in 1852, to Bathurst and Bissau in 1859, to Liberia in 1864, and to Sierra Leone in 1872. Strickland was, however, the first consul to *French West Africa.*

By 1883, the United States had established consular offices in several other regions of Africa: the Barbary States of Algiers, Tripoli, Tunis, and Tangier to the north, as well as Gabon, Luanda, Cape Town, Mauritius, Seychelles, Madagascar, and Zanzibar to the south. No evidence exists that Strickland corresponded with or knew his consular colleagues at these posts. Whereas today diplomats and consuls assigned to the same region or continent tend to work collegially, the situation during the colonial era was totally different. Diplomats and consuls would not have considered themselves to be colleagues; a modicum of unification would come only in 1924 when the Foreign Service was organized.

In the French colony of Senegal, Consul Strickland was not technically considered a diplomat. Diplomats were accredited to the government, and the seat of government was Paris, where the United States had a minister resident and a consul general. There were several U.S. consuls assigned to metropolitan France in Le Havre, Marseilles, Bordeaux, Lyons, La Rochelle, Nantes, Boulogne, and Nice. Strickland maintained relations with none of these appointees that we know of. He did send his initial report to the U.S. legation in Paris before he realized that his correspondence should be addressed directly to Washington.

In 1883, the African political realities of physical location and administrative authority were very different from those today. In Senegal, the consul was physically in Africa, but administratively in France. Senegal was a French colonial possession; Cape Verde

Islands belonged to Portugal; Sierra Leone and Bathurst were British. Colonization was still ongoing; few dreamed of decolonization or independence, which would come three-quarters of a century later.

An appointee as a consular officer had certain formalities to carry out. Following his appointment by the president and confirmation by the Senate, the consular officer took an oath of allegiance and executed a bond before a United States district attorney. Strickland carried out these formalities in Boston. The bond was duly deposited in the Department of Treasury in Washington.

The consular service in the nineteenth century had two main functions: to offer protection to American travelers and to supervise American shipping interests abroad. Since there were few American travelers to Senegal during Strickland's tenure, the second function consumed most of his time. He verified that ships' papers were in order; certified the health of the vessel, cargo, crew, and passengers; heard protests of captains and crew; took care of sailors in distress; received oaths from importers as to the value of cargo; and authenticated foreign documents for use in American business and courts. A consul was not expected to create or to maintain trade, but he was expected to facilitate it. With an eye always trained on merchandise entering and leaving port, he was in a fine position to advise potential traders on market opportunities.

Mention of the most common consular forms will help to introduce Strickland's specific consular duties. When a ship captain wished to record some shipping mishap, such as a bad storm, to protect him for insurance purposes against liability for eventual cargo damage, he "lodged a protest." Consular form no. 37 is called "mariner note of protest." Both ship captain and consul sign the document. This book contains an example of such a document on page 47.

The government had devised form no. 38, "mariner extended note of protest" for incidents whereby major mishaps required substantial description. In 1895, Captain Antonio Brito described the shipwreck of the schooner *Rebecca L. Evans* off the coast of Dakar where the surf was so high and the wind so fierce that the crew dismasted the ship to try to save her: the cargo of cattle started to swim ashore; the natives came on board to loot the ship; the bruised and exhausted crew remained on the wreck for four days before abandoning her.[5]

Form no. 74, which Strickland filled out a few times, was an oath of master to death or loss overboard at sea of a seaman or mariner. The form included the name of the sailor, date of death, and provenance of the vessel. For example, on January 29, 1902, a second mate on board the barkentine *Arlington* out of Boston drowned. The captain swore to this information with his signature and the consul signed. Form no. 90 gave the State Department specific details on rent and miscellaneous expenses per quarter, with accompanying vouchers.

Strickland filled out each quarter form no. 103 on the summary of business at the United States consulate. This form first requested numbers in several categories regarding vessels: number in port, number arriving, number departing, number remaining in port, tonnage arriving, tonnage departing, fees received, and expenses. Then the form included several categories of information regarding seamen: number in port at start of quarter, number arriving, number shipped, number deceased, number discharged, number deserted, number departed, and number in port at end of quarter.[6]

To inform the State Department on the frequency, itinerary, and cargo related to ship traffic, Strickland filled out consular form no. 120 each time an American vessel entered and exited the Gorée-Dakar port. During his twenty-three years as consul, he noted 256 vessel stops. Seventy-nine vessels made visits, with one, the *M. E. Higgins*, making sixty calls. Somewhat fewer than half of the calls were vessels coming from or going to the States. The majority were vessels used in the coastal trade from St. Louis at the mouth of the Senegal River in northern Senegal, down the coast to Bathurst, Bissau, Sierra Leone, and "The Rivers" or Rio Nuñez in French Guinea. These coastal voyages also stopped at different ports on Cape Verde Islands—Sal, Brava, Santiago, San Vicente—and at Rufisque across the bay from Gorée.

Peter Strickland's consular career lasted from December 20, 1883, when the U.S. Senate confirmed his recess appointment by President Chester Arthur, until July 25, 1906, when he retired under President Theodore Roosevelt. Strickland served under three other presidents: Grover Cleveland, Benjamin Harrison, and William

McKinley. He served ten Secretaries of State, including James G. Blaine, John Hay, and Elihu Root. While Strickland's longevity as a consul is unheard of today, it is far from being a record: Horatio Jones Sprague served fifty-three years as consul to Gibraltar from 1848 to 1901.[7]

Consuls general were encouraged to visit the consulates in their jurisdictions "for the purposes of inspection and report."[8] Strickland never received such a visit. Consuls would have to wait until 1906 to greet their first inspectors; the first such visit to Senegal took place in 1915, ten years after Strickland left. He was very much on his own.

As stipulated in 1881 consular regulations, Strickland directed his dispatches—spelled "despatches" at the time—to the assistant secretary of state. He sent 272 dispatches, amounting to 896 pages, written by hand. On March 10, 1904, he used a typewriter in a letter to the chief of the consular office in Washington, D.C. He must not have found this means of correspondence satisfactory, for he went right back to handwriting on March 15. The State Department had begun sending correspondence to consuls in typewritten form as early as 1881. Strickland hand copied his dispatches for his own consulate's records. Although his son George and daughter Mary copied some for him, most bear his handwriting.

The dispatches cover topics that the U.S. government routinely required information on, plus other personal concerns of the consul, such as benefits. Most of the pages deal with routine reports, covering military intelligence, colonial administrative development, commercial information, health epidemics, American ship traffic, and maintenance of the consulate.

Within the first year of his posting, Strickland compiled and sent to the State Department a succinct description of his territory in Senegal and of the region that surrounded it.

Geographically, French Senegal extends from the Great Desert to near Sierra Leone, embracing a section of Coast about six hundred miles in length, for the most part extremely fertile, and abounding with navigable Rivers which render access to the interior comparatively cheap and easy. Of these, the Senegal River is navigable for 600 miles during half of the year, and is being connected with the Niger by a Railroad Bafoulabe to Bamanakou which will give it the trade of the whole upper Niger valley. The other Rivers of importance are the Saloum, the Casamance, the Cassini, the Nunez, the Ponga, the Dubreka, and the Mallacore; all navigable for distances ranging from 10 to 150 miles. Sandwiched between the French sections of Coast are some English Settlements confined closely to the banks of the Gambia, which is a magnificent River navigable for 400 miles, and some Portuguese Settlements about Bulama, where there are also three fine Rivers each navigable for more than a hundred miles. The Commerce of both the English and Portuguese possessions is essentially under French control, and Goree-Dakar from its central position and accessibility to mail Steamers is the commercial emporium of the whole coast.

Of cities and towns. St.-Louis, built in handsome European style on an island in the Senegal River, is the capital, with a large commerce, and contains with its environs about 30,000 inhabitants. Goree-Dakar with their environs, including Rifisk in sight on the same Bay, contains fully 25000 inhabitants, and there are numerous towns further South in French Senegal which contain from one to five thousand inhabitants, all doing a thriving trade with Gorée (which is a free port) by means of Coasters ranging from 10 to 150 tons, many of them timbered with mahogany and rosewood which abounds at different places on the coast.[9]

Strickland considered Gorée-Dakar to have enormous potential to support vibrant commerce; he wanted to increase the American share of the pie. The French had managed to become the predominant commercial power on the coast, which included British as well as Portuguese colonial possessions. Strickland reported on the French presence in West Africa and on many other topics of particular interest to the Department of Commerce and Labor. This department through its Bureau of Manufactures often published Strickland's articles separately as consular reports worthy of wide circulation.[10]

The year 1883 marked the beginning of the Berlin Conference organized by Bismarck, at which European powers divided up much of the African continent, establishing borders, including those around Senegal. In April 1886 Strickland reported on fighting between the French military and about 8,000 Senegalese subjects in the town of Bakel on the Senegal River in eastern Senegal. Strickland was initially concerned that the conflict would have a negative impact on trade; later, he worried that several French had been killed. Bakel lay in an area, which produced gum arabic. Strickland concluded that the gum trade would be suspended as a result of the violent confrontations. Consequently, a popular export commodity from Senegal to the United States would be in short supply.

In November 1886 Strickland sent the State Department a Dakar newspaper article along with a dispatch regarding the death of the King of Cayor, Lat Dior. Lat Dior had fought against French penetration for over twenty-five years, until the French army killed him and seventy-eight of his followers in late October. Lat Dior later became a Senegalese national hero, immortalized in novels, film, drama, and radio.

Again, Strickland reacted principally to the death as an event that would adversely affect the peanut trade. However, he did recognize that Lat Dior had succumbed "while trying to defend himself from being exiled by foreigners, on the borders of his own country."[11] That is, the consul admits that Lat Dior was in his country and that the French were outsiders.

The State Department welcomed news on military activity from its overseas officers. In 1891, the French were building a new capital to replace Gorée: Dakar, on the mainland. They reinforced the battery on the island to protect the new harbor.

In consequence of Orders lately received from France, the Guns on the fortifications at Goree have been dismounted, and the fortifications themselves are being demolished with a view to reconstruct them on the most approved principles of modern military art. Twelve enormous guns are thus to be mounted in place of the lighter ones which until lately have been in use, and all the batteries on other parts of the Island will be discontinued. These outlying batteries were three in number and mounted in the aggregate twenty guns of about 6 ¾ inch caliber, rifled but muzzle-loading. . . . Goree commands the approaches to Dakar by Sea, and the work in progress will therefore be of the utmost importance in the defense of the latter place. And when the new naval station at Dakar is thus protected the constructions which are necessary to make it complete will be pushed forward with vigour.[12]

In 1898, the United States was at war with Spain. On June 1, the State Department sent a circular to consuls requesting information concerning the movements of Spanish war vessels. Strickland received the circular on June 28. Even in wartime, communications were slow to cross the ocean.[13] Spanish warships were frequent visitors to the port of Dakar. Consul Strickland used a code when reporting on Spanish naval activity. "Apple cormorant" meant "one gunboat." "Pear scorpion" signified "two torpedo craft."

In 1901, French authorities from Senegal and British authorities from The Gambia met in St. Louis to discuss how they could join forces to defeat an indigenous group of warriors who had killed some British along the Gambia River and escaped into French territory. The British dispatched a warship and with the French organized a cooperative expedition. Again, Strickland feared for the impact on trade. "I understand that these disturbances are likely to have a disastrous effect on the commerce of the Gambia Colony for at least this season."[14]

In 1904, Strickland reported a continual military buildup around Dakar, to the extent that commercial activities diminished. "Commercial business here is at the present moment much depressed, while the greatest activity prevails in Military and Naval circles. A large number of men are constantly employed raising fortifications, mounting guns, landing and storing ammunition, while target practice both from the shore batteries and from vessels is going forward to a greater extent than I have ever seen it here before."[15]

Later in 1904, Strickland reported on military activity during the Russo-Japanese War. The Russian Baltic fleet with five battleships, six cruisers, and a hospital ship stopped in Senegal to take on coal. To do this, they preferred to stay outside of French jurisdiction, about three and a half miles eastwards of Gorée, Strickland reported.[16] The Bay of Gorée offered a large sheltered area and obviated any need to go into port. Lighters from English steamers delivered coal to the Russian vessels. At night, all ships in the fleet would put on their searchlights and signal each other. Strickland commented that one had never seen such a magnificent nocturnal display of light in those waters. He further speculated that the Russian cruisers with three chimneys were actually transformed steamers from the Hamburg-America Line.

During the visit by the Baltic fleet, news spread in Dakar that a Russian officer had died of sunstroke. Apparently, the Russians had left the Baltic with winter clothing and no dress appropriate for the tropics. The Russians bought out Dakar stores of light clothing and casques. Strickland reported that he expected the fleet to go from Senegal to Japan to prevent that island from receiving supplies.

A significant reform in colonial administration took place during Consul Strickland's watch: the formation of the French West Africa federation, *AOF* (*Afrique Occidentale Française*). Strickland reported to Washington a decree making Dakar the capital of French West Africa.

> A cablegram has just arrived from Paris to the effect that according to a decree of the French Government the separate colonies of Senegal, Guinea, Ivory Coast, Dahomey, and the Soudan are to be presided over by a Governor-general whose place of residence will be at Dakar. Each colony will retain its Governor, but all Correspondence with the home Government will be addressed through the Governor-general at Dakar. The change will become operative in February next.[17]

Senegal would thus house two capitals: A governor would reside in St. Louis in the north, which remained the capital of the colony of Senegal. A governor-general would reside in Dakar and supervise the administration of five colonies, later expanded to include Mauritania and Niger. The governor-general would not move from Gorée to Dakar until 1907, however, when a new official residence was built.

Confusion naturally arose regarding the capitals in Senegal, especially as to the relationship between Gorée and Dakar. Not the least confused was the State Department. In an undated internal memo included in Strickland's microfilmed dispatches, a State Department official who signs "C." asked this question: "Please ask Consul to report whether Consulate is located at Goree or Dakar; where the Consulate should properly be located; which is the most prominent place commercially, and whether in his opinion the name should be changed from Goree-Dakar to Gorée or Dakar."[18]

Strickland may well have lived on Gorée Island for over twenty years by then and mentioned that fact many times in previous dispatches; however, State Department officials still were confused. The consul sent a dispatch to try to clarify the situation for them.

> I have the honor to report that for the next two years probably I do not think it will be advisable to change this consulate away from Gorée . . . . When the name Goree-Dakar was adopted the two places formed one municipality with the Government at Goree, but the two places are now separated in administration, although the center of Goree is not probably more than two miles from the commercial center of Dakar, and the two places are connected by a steam ferry-boat which makes six trips daily. . . . Dakar is doubtless the place where the Consulate should eventually be located. . . . The buildings I now occupy if situated in Dakar would let for at least $1500 a year, but here in Goree I pay scarcely half of that sum.[19]

The combined name "Gorée-Dakar" was a creation of the colonial administration when both localities formed part of the same municipality, in itself a source of confusion. Initially, Dakar was administratively part of Gorée; in time, Gorée became part of Dakar. Sometimes in his official correspondence on consulate letterhead, Strickland would cross out Dakar in the name "Gorée-Dakar."

Since Strickland was a businessman, he was keenly aware of Senegal's commercial importance. Many of his dispatches in the

1880s give details on trade in the natural harbor where he was posted.

> At this westernmost point of Africa, in sight of which a large part of the commerce of Europe passes going southerly we have one of the largest, cleanest, and safest harbors in the world: as easy of access by night as by day; no bar or other obstruction to impede its entrance and a depth of water sufficient for vessels of any size. Three cities are situated on different sides of this immense natural harbor, two of which are connected with the interior by a good Railroad which has been in successful operation for nearly four years through one hundred and forty miles of extent. From twenty to forty steamers a month, according to the season of the year, afford Goree-Dakar ample means of communication with Europe and the outside world, and the mail and telegraphic facilities are excellent. Rufisque, a city of about fifteen thousand inhabitants, on the east side of the Bay of Goree and within sight of the Consulate is illuminated by the electric light, and has a first-class iron wharf in process of construction one hundred and fifty meters in length. All of its principal streets are laid with tramways, over which merchandise as well as passengers are transported, and nothing is done in the primitive manner which was so prevalent twenty years ago. Dakar is a new city with elegant buildings, wide streets shaded with trees, and a large park which would do honor to any city within the tropics. Several War-vessels are almost constantly anchored before the town, and the band from the Admiral's ship plays in the Great Square quite often when the evenings are pleasant and other circumstances are favorable. Goree being a free-port is favorably situated for storing and transshipping cargoes that are intended for other parts of the coast, and consequently some of the largest firms in Senegal are here located. By means of small steamers and schooners goods received from Europe and other parts are distributed to all the small places between the Great Desert and Sierra Leone and the produce which is received in payment is brought here for transshipment in

larger vessels to Europe or to America. I am not able to state the exact amount of American trade with the French colony of Senegal, but counting tobacco which is received into all our ports by way of Europe, and produce in payment which goes back to America by way of Europe, I am reasonably sure that the figures would considerably exceed a million of dollars annually, which figures might also if we had more shipping and a less protective duty on peanuts be almost indefinitely increased.[20]

Strickland's vision of vibrant commercial traffic between the U.S. and Senegal never materialized. The European powers were making concentrated efforts to squeeze the United States out of any predominant trade position. Strickland wrote, "It is for the interest of all large European concerns to discourage as much as possible direct trade with America: hence they curtail their dealing with resident American Merchants and import such articles of American production as are absolutely needed in the prosecution of their business either through their correspondents in Europe or if the articles be bulky <u>sometimes</u> [Strickland's underline] direct from America."[21]

In the 1870s, Strickland had reported to his shipping agent in Boston that the French mercantile houses gave him their business on the west coast of Africa. In a decade, the French through their agents in New York and Boston were dealing directly with American firms rather than working through American agents located in West Africa.

There was a concomitant decrease in the number of American ships coming to West African ports. In 1886, Strickland reported that at the time of his writing there were about ten thousand tons of ship cargo in port with about five hundred of that being American.[22]

By the mid-1890s, high protective tariffs in the United States and French Africa diminished trade between the two regions. The McKinley tariff, passed in 1895, affected the peanut trade with West Africa. Strickland reported a new "discriminating duty of seven per cent, which is levied by the Government of this Colony and I believe by the Governments of nearly all the French Colonies, on all imported goods that are not produced in France. This tariff came into existence in just three months after our own McKinley tariff began to take effect, and very quickly nearly extinguished nearly all that before remained of direct American Commerce this way."[23]

The State Department depended on consuls to report on health conditions abroad. The consul notified Washington when American seamen died within his jurisdiction. For example, "It becomes my painful duty to report to you the death from Typhoid Malaria Fever in Hospital at Gorée of two seamen from the Brig *Lucy C. Snow*."[24] Strickland lost his vice-consul, Charles Armand, due to "blood poisoning from malaria." He reported a twenty-three-day quarantine at the mouth of the Niger River due to a yellow fever epidemic in 1891.

In 1893, Strickland reported a cholera epidemic with twenty deaths per day in Dakar. He judged it urgent enough to send a cable to the Department of State: "Cholera Senegal Strickland."[25] Washington received it the same day, and was grateful. When Dakar was declared free of cholera five months later, Strickland also reported that fact to the State Department.

In June of 1900, another outbreak of yellow fever occurred in Senegal. Strickland reported the fact in a dispatch, explaining that he did not telegraph the news because an epidemic had not been declared. He weighed the necessity of using the more expensive cable to expedite his message. Even without a declared epidemic, however, steamships to and from Europe bypassed Dakar for fear of contagion. An epidemic was eventually declared: 92 percent of those who caught the disease died. Strickland's daughter Mary caught yellow fever and he was initially afraid she might not survive.

In 1905, in one of his last dispatches from Senegal, Strickland reported that sewers were being laid in Dakar. Improvement in the sanitary conditions in the city would limit the incidence of disease.

Since it was Strickland's primary duty to monitor, facilitate, and encourage American ship traffic, many of his dispatches refer to American ships that called at Gorée-Dakar. The messages address a variety of topics such as ship movement, communications, untoward captain or sailor behavior, shipwrecks, damaged cargo, and sale of a vessel.

The first vessel Strickland informed Washington about was a schooner from Boston, the *Ripple*. Its owner, Francis C. Butman of

Boston, owned several sailing vessels, which he employed for trade on the west coast of Africa.

The matter which Strickland drew to the State Department's attention was the nationality of the crew. Butman had replaced the original crew that sailed from Boston with Africans, in an effort to avoid the health problems to which white crewmembers were susceptible. Strickland signed the discharge of the original crew and settled with them. They returned to Boston in another of Butman's vessels.[26]

A routine report Strickland made on ship movements would look like this: "Bark *Jennie Cushman* of Boston arrived here from that port May 20th, discharged the most of her cargo, took on board 8227 dry hides and sailed for Boston via Santiago [Cape Verde Islands] May 28. A Consular Certificate No. 3 was given for the Hides and the triplicate sent to the Collector in Boston, as provided by law."[27]

An incident of sailor behavior that Strickland reported involved a crewmember who drew a knife on his captain. Strickland had a talk with the sailor and advised the captain to take the man back to Boston in irons, or release him if he were deemed repentant. Strickland wrote,

> I examined the man on board and found that he had no cause whatever for complaint. He is, in my opinion, a dangerous character, and the exemplary punishment of a few such by our Courts would do much to promote discipline and safety in our vessels. But unfortunately there is practically no way to prosecute them. The Officers of vessels are generally poor men who cannot afford the delays of the law, and will let the worst of criminals escape rather than appear against them.[28]

Strickland had seen many incidents of violence on the part of sailors. Now that he was a consul and no longer common sailor or ship officer, his role was to collect information on the case, and make a judgment.

The consul also reported when an American ship changed hands and nationalities. More than once, French trading companies purchased American ships for their own use. Such a report reads:

"The Schr *M. E. Higgins,* of Boston, Mass. of the burden of 89.76 tons, has been sold by the legal representatives of F. C. Butman, Esq. her former owner, to the 'Compagnie Francaise de l'Afrique Occidentale,' of Marseilles, and that henceforth she will be under the French flag."[29] While Strickland refrained from any comment in his dispatch, the *M. E. Higgins* was the vessel from which his son George fell when he drowned five years earlier.

Shipwrecks within Consul Strickland's jurisdiction were infrequent events; when they occurred, however, they involved considerable time, work, and financial resources. In April 1895 the schooner *Rebecca L. Evans* of Boston went down fourteen kilometers northeast of the Cape Verde peninsula. The cargo consisted of live cattle and fruit. When Strickland first heard of it, he learned that the crew of five was safe and encamped on the wreck.[30]

Strickland had to decide what to do with the wreck from both a practical and a legal perspective. On May 6, 1895, on consular stationery, he made a proposal to the French authorities. The consul is writing on behalf of the captain.

> I have the honor to bring to your notice that Antonio H. Brito, master of the American Schr *Rebecca L. Evans,* lately wrecked on the Coast N.E. of Cape de Verde, having found it impossible to save anything further from the wreck, desires to relinquish the care of it to the Colonial authorities; to be sold by them at Public Auction if anything is likely to accrue from such a proceeding commensurate with the expense. No funds are available to pay for anything which may be done with a view to save more from the wrecked property, but the Colonial Government is hereby authorized to order an auction of the wreck if in its judgment the proceeds shall equal the expenses, and if there should remain a net balance it can be paid in at this Consulate for the benefit of whom it may concern.[31]

Strickland wrote the May 6 letter by hand and in English. There is no indication that he conveyed a French translation. He counted on the French authorities to figure out the contents of his official communications. This official letter is reproduced on page 109.

Another matter to settle was the crew's future. Strickland informed the State Department that since there were no longer regular sailings of American vessels from the United States directly to Gorée-Dakar, he might have to secure passage for the crew in steamers through Europe to return to the States.[32] He feared the heavy cost. The problem was resolved, however, when the five crewmembers, all of Portuguese extraction, agreed to be transported only as far as to the Cape Verde Islands. Strickland reported as his expenses $183.40 for passage of five seamen to Cape Verde Islands and for lodging and food from April 25 to May 29. It took over a month to settle the issues raised by the shipwreck, the disposal of the cargo, lodging and feeding for the crew, and its onward passage.

By contrast, a shipwreck occurring four years later appeared to require fewer resources. Strickland again mentions the use of a public auction. "Loss of Schooner *Oliver Cromwell* of New-Bedford" was the subject of a dispatch concerning a vessel stranded on a reef of sunken rocks during a tempest. The *Oliver Cromwell* sold at public auction for less than $400."[33]

Strickland also played an official role in cases of damage to ship cargo. A consul's signature required in claims requests to insurance agents. One such case is a voyage of the three-masted schooner *Jeanie Lippitt* from Boston in 1901. Its captain, H. H. Chase, feared reimbursement problems when bad weather caused part of the tobacco cargo to get wet. Strickland explained the situation to the State Department, "Tobacco is insured in such a way that it is questionable if the insured in this case can get reimbursement from the insurers."[34]

On occasion, Strickland intervened in cases where Americans were traveling to other countries and passing through Senegal. Strickland advanced money to a destitute American missionary couple on their way to Liberia. He subsequently requested reimbursement from the State Department. The answer finally came: "the department regrets that there is no fund from which you can be reimbursed the amount expended by you recently in relieving two destitute American missionaries."[35] The incident reveals that Consul Strickland confronted situations where he made an independent judgment to help an American in distress, regardless of reimbursement. Actually, in this case, the story was not over. The missionary died soon after his arrival in Liberia. His wife nevertheless repaid her debt to Strickland, who sent back the money.

As the only American consul in French West Africa, Strickland had to deal with issues regarding U.S. citizens in territories outside of Senegal. In 1904, a seaman was hospitalized in Conakry, Guinea. When he was better, the French authorities in Conakry wrote an official letter to Strickland about the seaman and sent him to Gorée.[36]

In 1904, the State Department requested that Strickland obtain permission from the French to perform consular services temporarily for the Republic of Panama, until the new Republic could hire and train its own. Panama had gained its independence from Colombia on Nov. 3, 1903. The same year, Panama signed a treaty authorizing the United States to build and operate the waterway that would become the Panama Canal. The relationship with Panama in Central America had suddenly become a vital interest for the United States.

On April 18, 1904, Strickland wrote to the governor-general of French West Africa asking for his consent that the American consul in Senegal represent Panama. The letter, found in the National Archives in Dakar, is reproduced in this book on page 110.[37] The French authorities in Dakar forwarded the request to Paris. Strickland eventually heard back that before his request met with approval he should produce an exequatur, a document recognizing a foreign consular officer. Strickland consulted with the State Department. It was agreed that since Strickland would not be representing Panama's interests permanently an exequatur was not needed. The French lieutenant governor of Senegal in St. Louis Camille Guy wrote Strickland giving this permission.[38] On August 13, 1904, Strickland wrote to the governor-general again to acknowledge French agreement that Strickland "perform consular services when necessary for the Republic of Panama throughout the French possessions in West Africa until the said Republic shall appoint its own consuls."[39]

It is not clear that Strickland ever conducted any consular business for Panama. He feared that destitute seamen from Panama would present themselves at his door asking for assistance, as had others from Cuba, Chile, Uruguay, and several other countries in Central and South America. At any rate, the hand of American colonialism in Central America had reached out as far away as West Africa.

Strickland conducted consular business from a room eighteen square feet in size on the second floor of the quarters he rented as a residence. He was required to justify each expenditure for the consulate. Generally he would pay for the items and wait for reimbursement, as detailed in his records. "I have expended for a new hardpine Cabinet, of large size, and constructed with a special view to the preservation of its contents, fifty dollars; for a new well painted mast, made from the heart of a new spruce spar 38 ft long and securely fastened to the wall, twenty-five dollars."[40] Ten years later, Strickland asked permission to spend $10 to repair the flagpole and to buy a bureau for $15 and a bookcase for $12. He included a photograph of the bookcase with the dispatch. The State Department saved the photo and pasted it into the album holding dispatches. Behind the chairs in the photo, one can clearly make out the pilasters on the balcony on the house Strickland rented from Léopold Angrand.

As anyone living in the tropics knows, insects will take over bureaus and bookcases and bore through wood as well as paper and cloth. Strickland periodically fumigated the furniture containing his consular records. Although he kept his material relatively clean, in 1901 he received three boxes of consular items from the consulate in Bathurst that had just closed. He counted seventy-three books, "but many of them have been eaten more or less by roaches and other vermin."[41]

Controllers from the Treasury Department regularly audited Consul Strickland's reports, almost always finding the accounts balanced. In 1891, however, they caught him off by a dollar and called him on it. Strickland had charged a captain one dollar for a document certifying the appointment of a new master. The correct fee for this service should have been two dollars.[42]

When Strickland was to leave Senegal, perhaps not to return, the State Department directed him to send all his archives to the American consulate in neighboring Sierra Leone.[43] He considered this a bizarre choice of destination, as he later confided in his correspondence.

Strickland was authorized to hire a deputy, allowing himself the freedom to go on leave or to visit the regions under his jurisdiction and know that consular matters would be handled during his absence. He had only three vice-consuls during his long stay on Gorée. Strickland would propose a name and justify his choice among the candidates he had considered; the State Department accepted each time.

The first vice-consul was the Frenchman Charles Armand. While the idea of an American consul selecting a French deputy would be unthinkable today, Strickland had good reason for his choice. He knew Armand well, having employed him in his import-export business since 1880, when they both were on the payroll of the Boston ship owner Matthew Bartlett. One drawback that Strickland mentioned to the State Department was Armand's imperfect mastery of English. After serving only eighteen months, Armand died from malaria while on a steamer taking him to France.

One other American was available for the job of vice-consul: George Strickland. Peter Strickland had felt uncomfortable proposing his own son for the post. His search had turned up only one other candidate, the mayor of Gorée. "It is not perhaps delicate for a father to recommend his own Son, and I shall not do so only to state facts which under the circumstances may be acted on or not as the department shall think proper. He is 21 years of age, was born in New London, Connecticut, has been educated both Classically and Commercially, writes an elegant hand and can both speak and write the French language with facility. He was with me here all of last season and has altogether lived as many as three years in Africa."[44]

It was a logical choice, which the State Department readily approved. Strickland wrote later that his son might have been the youngest vice-consul ever appointed.[45] The State Department does not keep age records and could not verify this claim.

Peter Strickland had taken pains to give his son a first-class education. He enrolled sixteen-year-old George in Adams Academy, an elite boys' private school in Quincy, near Boston. Strickland was bound to be impressed by the credentials of the Academy's headmaster. Son of Massachusetts governor and respected orator Edward Everett, William Everett was a Harvard graduate, a Latin professor, a trained lawyer, and a practicing Unitarian minister.

After several years as headmaster, William Everett realized that student records were deficient. On February 1, 1888, he addressed a letter to all known former pupils. It began with the impersonal passive voice of the day, "It is desired to form a complete list of the persons who have attended Adams Academy since its opening in 1872."[46] The letter ended with a solicitation to provide information such as name, address, subsequent institutions of learning, and date of decease in case of that event.

The letter was sent to the Strickland home on Neponset Avenue in neighboring Dorchester. George was on the books as having attended the Academy from 1880 until 1882. Mrs. Mary Louise Strickland or her daughter Grace would have opened the letter, as George, Mary, and father Peter were in Senegal. Although it is not known whether the Stricklands responded to the Academy's letter, the grim fact is that George Strickland died the same week, on February 7, 1888, at age twenty-three.

The circumstances of George Strickland's death are unusual if not mysterious, in spite of the straightforward and sober dispatch, which the deceased's father sent to the State Department on February 20.

> I have the extreme unhappiness to inform you of the death by drowning on the evening of the 7th instant of my only Son, Mr. George Strickland, the Vice-Consul. He embarked for Saint-Louis taking passage in the Schooner *M. E. Higgins*, on the morning of the 6th instant, and when the vessel was about fifteen miles NW of Cape de Verde Light he accidentally fell from one of the rails where he was sitting without apprehension of danger into the sea. A boat was launched instantly and every effort made to save him but he sank finally before he could be picked up. It was about eight o'clock in the evening when the accident occurred. The vessel was kept as near as possible to the spot all of that night and the most of the next day when, finding no trace of anything she returned to Goree with the sad news.
>
> Great sympathy has been manifested by the Officers of the Government and by the people generally in the Colony.

All flags at Goree, both afloat and ashore, were displayed at half-mast on the day the news arrived, the Governor telegraphed expressions of sympathy from St. Louis, and Admiral Ribell of the French Frigate *Arethuse*: everything possible has been done by a kind people that would tend to mitigate a grief, but this is the kind which inevitably takes shape for enduring reasons.

The deceased expected to visit America in a few months. He was only 23 years of age and had a large circle of acquaintances. His sister aged 19 came out here with me in November and is inconsolable at his loss.[47]

George Strickland was appointed vice-consul on April 12, 1885, five days short of his twenty-first birthday. He had served less than three years when he died. The State Department first heard of the accidental drowning from Paris, and sent a letter of condolence on March 18, 1888.

The Department receives with deep regret the sad intelligence of the death by drowning of your son, Vice-Consul George Strickland which has been communicated in dispatch No. 563 from the Legation at Paris.

As it appears by the same dispatch that this accident may make it necessary for you to come home, leave of absence for this purpose is hereby granted you subject to the requirements of the statutes and regulations.[48]

A drowning accident at sea leads one to ask initially at least four questions: Was the weather bad? Was this a treacherous area for maritime navigation? Was the victim accustomed to sea voyages? Could the victim swim? Nothing in Strickland's dispatches, journal, or in the record of the voyage gives any indication of foul weather on February 7. The accident took place within fifteen miles northwest of the Cape Verde lighthouse, familiarly called *Phare des mamelles* off Dakar. Built in 1864 by the French, it is the second most powerful lighthouse in Africa, casting its beam as far away as thirty miles. The shoreline is dangerously rocky, but a path northwest from the lighthouse as indicated in the consul's dispatch would have put the vessel well out to sea.

George Strickland fell from the railing of a ninety-ton schooner, the *M. E. Higgins*. The vessel was eighty feet long, twenty-three feet wide, with an eight-foot draft. The owner of the vessel, Francis C. Butman, was the Boston merchant who had employed Peter Strickland to conduct commercial voyages along the coast of West Africa. Ironically, before sailing out of Boston, the *M. E. Higgins* hailed from New London, where its captain was Benjamin N. Rogers, a distant relative of Mrs. Peter Strickland.

It would have been a fall of perhaps ten feet from the railing. In February off the coast of Dakar, the weather is cold and windy at night. In particular, at eight o'clock in the evening, it would have been pitch black. Even with some light from the lighthouse fifteen miles away, it would have been difficult on a February night to make out anyone fallen into those waters.

It is not clear to what extent George Strickland knew how to swim. However, George, like his father, was a sea captain.[49] Although nowhere in Strickland's correspondence or journal does he speak of his son as being a shipmaster, files at the U.S. National Archives show that George Strickland first commanded a vessel in March 1886 from Bathurst to Gorée-Dakar to Bissau. The vessel was named the *M. E. Higgins*.

From March 1886 until the fateful voyage in February 1888, George Strickland served as master on eighteen voyages of the ship. He knew the vessel well. These were coastal trips from St. Louis in northern Senegal to the Rio Nuñez in Guinea and as far west as to the Cape Verde Islands. On these voyages, the ship's crew consisted of from four to nine members. The crew was all from Senegal and Cape Verde, and virtually the same individuals on each of the voyages of the *M. E. Higgins*. On the trips, cargoes consisted typically of animal hides and rubber headed for the United States, and American goods such as tobacco and lumber for sale along the West African coast.

George Strickland was far from being a novice on a coastal sailing vessel plying the seas in West Africa. Accidents do happen, but falling from a ship's railing appears a highly unusual event. At any rate, the loss of his only son must have taken an enormous toll on Peter Strickland. He had been grooming his son to take over his business on the coast. Peter had bought property in Dakar, which could have served as a base for the younger Strickland. The father's hopes and dreams were dashed in the drowning accident.

An additional question pertains to George Strickland's duties as vice-consul: what did he accomplish? He helped his father in concrete ways and in giving him peace of mind when the consul was absent. He recopied in the consulate's own record book dispatches no. 38 through 65 for his father's signature. In fact, he spent his last New Year's Day, January 1, 1888, recopying his father's dispatches. The consul paid George three hundred francs a month for his services.

Replacing his father when Peter went on leave to America, George had to respond to all the same solicitations and petitions regarding American shipping as did the consul. On one occasion, the State Department commended George for his handling of a case, which came up during his father's absence from post. The American consul general in Liberia was incensed at having to suffer quarantine in a French port while aboard a British steamer headed for England. George tactfully tried to pacify the official. On another occasion, the State department rejected reimbursement of a $1.00 fee George had paid the Portuguese consul for a crew-list. State explained that an American vessel was not involved and the expense could not be justified.

Another time, George reported in a five-page letter to the State Department an episode where a Boston shipmaster had neglected to deposit his papers at the consulate. George referred the case to Washington for possible censure, pointing out that at times of yellow fever or smallpox epidemics the captain's arrogant behavior could have been costly.

George Strickland communicated with the State Department more often than his father did, writing and signing dispatches nos. 66 through 82 under his own name. George wrote these dispatches over the period July 6, 1887 through Jan. 1, 1888, when Peter Strickland was on leave. Following these seventeen dispatches is no. 83, written on Feb. 20, 1888 in the consul's hand, describing his son's death by drowning.

George Strickland's body was never found. The father wrote an epitaph for his son that appears on the family monument in the Strickland plot in New London, next to the graves of the other family members. The epitaph reads, "George Strickland, born in New London April 17, 1864. He was vice consul of the United States of America for French West Africa at the time of his death which occurred accidentally by drowning within the district of his consulate. February 7, 1888."

George's voyage from Gorée to St. Louis, Senegal on the *M. E. Higgins* would have had a commercial motive, although perhaps because of the accident the voyage was not written up in the consular record of ship visits. On this particular voyage, there is no record of the names of the crewmembers or of the nature of the cargo.

Strickland's third vice-consul was René Potin, approved by the State Department on May 3, 1888. Later, Strickland sent to the State Department Potin's bond, which was forwarded to the Department of the Treasury.

When Strickland did not have a vice-consul to replace him, and he received permission from the State Department to return to the United States on leave, he closed the consulate. In 1889, he wryly wrote to the Department, "I cannot for the beggarly pittance in fees which accrue to the Consulate here during the Rains find any-one willing to take my place. I see no remedy therefore but to close the Consulate until next Nov."[50] Sometimes, he sent notices to relevant officials in the French administration with directions that sea captains seeking a bill of health should get certification from two local merchants that the U. S. consulate was closed.

The consul interspersed his informative dispatches with sporadic expressions of personal needs. In twenty-three years, he asked for only three items: a vacation, a salary, and a new passport.

The State Department sent Strickland's passport to him in Boston before he sailed out in 1883. Fourteen years later, it occurred to Strickland that perhaps he should have a new one. He made a request in his polite indirect way. "I expect to embark (health wholly restored) on the Bark *Charles F. Ward* about the 20th of this month. My passport dates back more than a dozen years and perhaps it will be thought proper by the Department that I shall be furnished with a new one."[51] The Department agreed, but charged the consul for it. "Under the law a fee of one dollar is charged for all passports. Upon the receipt of this amount, a special passport will be sent to you."[52]

In those days, leaves of absence were very different from the ones offered in the modern-day consular service. Nowadays leave is based on a certain number of days—according to one's longevity in the service—annually which should be taken or otherwise forfeited. In Strickland's day, a consul requested leave when he felt he needed it. Leaves were initially for sixty days. If a consul needed more time off he submitted a justification. In Strickland's case, the Department acquiesced with a second sixty-day period of leave, "should your health require an extension of the time."[53] Strickland's leaves lasted five or six months, but took place only every five or six years. The period Strickland preferred to avoid in Senegal was from June to November, the rainy mosquito season when health hazards were at their highest.

Typically, Strickland would offer medical reasons to justify his leave. His request in 1897 is a good example. "Having passed six rainy seasons in succession here now, the French Colonial Doctors are unanimous in their opinion that my absence should be protracted for my own safety in the future to at least five or six months."[54] The department concurred in the request, but the answer took over two months in reaching the consul.

The question of putting the Gorée-Dakar consulate on a salary basis became a bone of contention throughout Peter Strickland's tenure. He pleaded for a salary for twenty years. When State finally agreed, a tired and ill Strickland resigned from the service.

When Peter Strickland joined the consular corps, he was sent a six-hundred-page set of regulations. During his years as consul, this guide would be updated twice, in 1890 and 1896. A major revision was issued in 1906, shortly after Strickland left the service. A main distinction in those days was whether the consular position was salaried or not. Why would one accept a nonsalaried position? It was possible then to earn a living as a businessman and be a consul. Today, a consul is a paid professional and such a conflict of interest would not be allowed.

In the late 1800s, there were over fifteen different "classes" of consuls, rising from consular clerk to consul general. One class of consul received a salary of $1,000 (or more) per annum, and could not engage in business. A second class of consul could engage in business. Some were salaried at a level below $1,000; others were not salaried but were allowed to keep the fees they received for their services. Strickland belonged to this last category. Fees were low and would not permit one to make a living. For example, to certify an invoice before a consul when an American vessel left port, a shipmaster would pay the consulate a fee of $2.50. Strickland would obtain about $200 a year from fees.

Strickland approached the State Department first in March 1886 with a timid, "pardon me." He extolled the commercial possibilities for the United States in West Africa and regretted that the American share of the trade was so meager. He suggested a minimum of $700 as a salary with no fees but with the possibility of conducting business.

> Pardon me for suggesting that I believe the whole Fee System is one calculated to weaken the moral sense of both Shipmasters and Consular Officers. Scores of Masters would approve of anything to gain the connivance of a Consular Officer on some point they wished to carry and have fees for pretended services multiplied almost indefinitely to increase his demand against the Government. Seven hundred dollars without fees, and a right to do business is as small a sum as would support a Consulate here.[55]

Strickland received no response. In April 1888, he pointed again to the magnificent natural harbor that Gorée-Dakar offered on the strategic westernmost tip of Africa. He had heard talk that the consulates on Cape Verde Islands, in Bathurst, The Gambia, and in Freetown, Sierra Leone were to be salaried, and he wondered: what about me?

This time, the consul's justification appeared to meet with some receptivity in Washington. A noted filed with dispatch no. 87 in the consul's microfilmed messages from Gorée-Dakar reads, "Dept regards Mr. Strickland's suggestions as worthy of consideration."[56] State explained that it submitted its consulate salary requests to the Foreign Affairs Committee at the House of Representatives.

Peter Strickland showed his appreciation for the favorable inclination by writing, "I am much gratified to know that my request for this Consulate to be placed on a salaried basis will receive due consideration in the Autumn of the present year."[57] Thinking it was only a matter of time, Strickland thought he should suggest an updated figure for a salary, and used a new argument. In order to attract a good vice-consul, he argued, a salary of $2,500 would be appropriate.[58]

Strickland heard in early 1892 that "the Secretary of State has recommended a salary of $1000 a year be granted for the maintenance of this Consulate."[59] The amount was not what Strickland had hoped, but it was something. In 1893, he introduced another reason why he desired a salary: he was supporting his family in Boston.[60] In 1894, he learned of the "lack of an appropriation on the part of Congress,"[61] due to "the present depression at home." Strickland would never get a consular salary.

In 1896, the consul alerted the State Department to the fact that England paid its consul a handsome salary in Dakar. This year marked a full decade since Strickland's initial request; "the commercial importance of this Colony is immensely greater than when the Consulate was first established. England, which had no greater interests here than what the United States might have, gives her Consul here one thousands pounds annually. I have several times asked for one fifty of this sum with the right to do business, but so far without success."[62] It is also true that the British government prohibited its consuls from commercial activity.

By January 1897, Strickland had waited over two months for the department to approve his leave, after having spent six consecutive years in the colony. With no answer about his leave request, and a decade of disappointments regarding a salaried position, no wonder that Strickland was less than enthused to receive a package containing a new set of consular regulations, 871 pages of them. "I have the honor to acknowledge the receipt of a copy of the New Consular Regulations, which shall have my full attention as soon as I can get time for the purpose."[63]

The new year reminded Strickland that his European peers were much better taken care of by their home offices than he was. Strickland informed Washington that London paid out 3,000 francs to rent an excellent residence for the British consul in Dakar.[64] No response came from Washington.

In 1903, the year marking two decades of Peter Strickland's service as consul at Gorée-Dakar, the State Department came to a conclusion about that consulate—not that it should become a salaried post, but that it should be closed. As justification, the department used Strickland's own report on the significant decline of American business activity in French West Africa. On March 7, 1903, the consular office expressed its assessment in these terms: "There is so little business done at Goree-Dakar that no hardship is likely to result from the closing of the office."[65]

Two years later, in 1905, Strickland decided to leave Senegal. He announced his intention to give up his rented quarters, including the room that served for the consulate.[66] In a rare telegram (omitting commas to save money), the State Department gave him instructions on how to close the consulate. "Ship records only. Sell mast safe furniture. Remit proceeds."[67] Strickland was to send the archives to the consulate in Sierra Leone, which he did. Strickland left Gorée with his daughter on July 21, carrying the consular dies and stamps with him to America. In his last dispatch, Strickland confirmed that he would send the seals and stamps from Boston to Washington.[68] He also confirmed that he would spend the winter in Boston with permission of the State Department, his first winter in twenty-five years.

Over a year after Strickland's return to the United States—on May 5, 1906—very curiously, the State Department sent him a dispatch to Gorée. The contents informed him that the consulate was being put on a salary basis for $2,000 a year: Would Strickland be interested in resuming duty on these terms?[69]

Strickland inquired of the State Department regarding the question of his business interests. He had already agreed to work for the Luckett-Wake Tobacco Company in Tennessee on a commission basis until 1908. State responded that the $2,000 salary would be incompatible with a continuation of his business interests. Strickland therefore determined that he would not be interested. He resigned from the consular service on July 25, 1906.

The successor to Peter Strickland as consul was William James Yerby (1867–1950), an African-American physician from Memphis, Tennessee. Yerby did not arrive in Senegal until 1915; the post was vacant for ten years. Yerby had been consul in nearby Sierra Leone from 1906. He did not establish residence on Gorée Island, but in Dakar; he opened a new consulate where he remained until 1924.

7

Retiree in Dorchester

P Strickland
Neponset Avenue
Dorchester district
Dublin
Massachusetts

When Consul Peter Strickland packed up his things and left Gorée with daughter Mary on July 21, 1905, he had not yet decided whether he would return to Africa. He had requested a leave of absence rather than a termination from government service. Strickland still harbored hopes of receiving a salary for his consular services, after two decades of attempting to obtain one.

On July 1, he had vacated the consulate and residence he had occupied for a quarter of a century. The month of June had seen an increase in the cases of yellow fever in Senegal and Strickland was anxious. The French steamers leaving Dakar were crowded with European families eager to leave the tropics.

Strickland had just turned over his import-export business to a French firm, Maurel & Frères. He had said his goodbyes in St. Louis, Rufisque, Dakar, and Gorée. He paid his staff their salaries. Carlo had put a fresh coat of paint on the trunks he would take to Boston.

Peter and Mary Strickland stepped onto the French steamer *La Cordillère* on July 21 and arrived in Bordeaux ten days later. Strickland felt ill. They continued by train, reaching Paris on August 12. After crossing the Channel on September 22, they boarded the White Star steamer RMS *Republic* in Liverpool. *Republic* was the flagship of the White Star's Liverpool-Boston service.[1] After a voyage of eight days, they were home in Dorchester.

What a contrast between the modest sailing vessels of Strickland's earlier voyages and the luxurious style of the ship in which he was returning to America. Forty years earlier, he had sailed from Boston to Gorée on the schooner *Indian Queen*, a 118-ton vessel seventy-eight feet long. In contrast, the steamer RMS *Republic* weighed 15,385 tons and was 570 feet long. Strickland wrote admiringly of the voyage. "We had a fine passage from Liverpool, and the immense Steamer moved so steadily that the tables in the saloon were set every day as if on shore, and scarcely a person was sea-sick. We had about 1200 passengers, many of them going to America for the first time to become Americans."[2]

In a sense, the two Stricklands were going to the States to renew their American roots. Both had spent more than half of their lives in West Africa. How would they adapt to their home country?

The first adaptation would be the reunion with family. Mr. and Mrs. Strickland were reunited on September 30, 1905, after twenty-five years of living apart. They had known terrible family tragedy: both of their sons had died. The last-born child, Grace, who had lived most of her life with her mother in Dorchester, was seriously ill with diphtheria. Her father considered her mentally unstable. The next year she too would die, at age thirty-one.

Back in West Africa in 1904, Strickland had described in his journal a fitful night he had spent visualizing his wife and daughter Grace in Dorchester. "Felt ill again at night and did not sleep well. Ordinarily I do sleep well, and the nights pass rapidly away. Last night all kinds of disagreeable subjects came up for reflection, and I seemingly could not prevent it. I pictured to myself a dreadful state of affairs at home, the development of the sad conditions, which prevailed there when I left. I fancied Grace more insane than she appeared to be then, and quite intractable. I was very much worried about what to do but about midnight I did get asleep and slept until 5:00 A.M."[3]

Strickland wrote his former neighbor in Gorée, Claude Potin, in early 1907, "Grace died on the 20th of December, and on account of our being obliged to carry her to another state for burial, her corpse was with us embalmed until Dec. 27th. We then took her to New-London. . . . I am very glad I was not away when my daughter died. Grace had not enjoyed good health since she had diphtheria more than a dozen years ago. A large tumor finally developed near her right arm which had to be removed by a surgeon and she died about a week after the operation. She spent about six months in Gorée when she was a child."[4]

A letter from Dorchester written in French the same day to another Gorée business colleague, Gabriel Escarpit, offers additional insights as to the relationship of his daughter's illness to his professional decisions. Strickland writes that after Grace's death, Christmas was a joyless celebration. Then he admits that it was partly on her account that he did not agree to return to the consulate. In addition, he ventured, correctly, that he would never again leave the United States.[5]

Peter Strickland's relationship with his wife Mary Louise Rogers had deteriorated over the years of their long separation. The idea of their marrying had clearly come from Peter's brother Henry and his wife, Mary Louise's sister Martha, back in 1860. They encouraged the match, and Peter agreed that it was a good idea. There is no evidence that he considered marrying anyone else. The Strickland and the Rogers families had previously intermarried in New London.

Mary Louise frequently saw members of the Rogers family in New London during the first ten years of her marriage to ease the transition into married status, but during the period 1861–1871, her sailor husband Peter was often away serving in the merchant marine. When he returned to New London between assignments, the pair spent a lot of time together. They went on long walks, up to ten miles: Peter mentioned with pride that many other ladies would tire after one mile. In the winter, they went skating.

The year 1863 was devastating for Mary Louise. During her husband's second absence from home since the birth of their child, the boy died of bronchitis at the age of ten months. On Christmas Eve 1863, Peter confided in his journal, "I am not well adapted to a sea-faring life in the respect that I love my home and friends better than many others do and it is very hard for me not to have them with me constantly."[6]

Peter's first trip to Africa took place in 1864. Although he had argued in several of his journal entries that adopting a merchant life on the African coast made little sense, that is exactly what he eventually did. In 1870, Strickland bought a home in Dorchester, as he had concluded that New London shipping offered him fewer merchant marine job possibilities. Mary Louise set up house in the Boston area where she knew nobody. By 1870, she had two children, George and Mary.

Peter's first long-term assignment to West Africa was to the Portuguese colony of Bissau (now independent Guinea Bissau), south of Senegal. He persuaded his wife Mary Louise to come to Africa while he lived there. She shared his African life for about three years, and on August 20, 1880, returned on the *Zingarella* to Dorchester, never again to travel to Africa. We have an idea why she did not—the health hazard of malaria. Peter's correspondence during the Bissau years gives hints that "Mrs. S.," as her husband called her, was ill. In 1900, Strickland wrote a medical doctor friend, explaining. "I lived in Bissau with a part of my family for nearly three years, but the results were not good, and I should not like to do the same thing again. We all suffered more or less from fever, and I do not think that any of us have ever yet fully recovered from the effects of it. It seems to me that it makes Europeans grow old very fast to live in countries which so abound in malaria."[7] Peter nevertheless would spend most of the following twenty-five years in West Africa.

Of the 2,000 letters Strickland copied into his letter-books, few are to his family. The letters to Mary Louise all begin "My dearest wife" and end "Your loving husband." These were common formulas of the day. His letters to her generally addressed financial concerns. Throughout all the years he was in Africa, he sent her money drafts. In one instance, his message showed how much he missed her physically. "I need you to make me entirely happy, your arms and lips I mean."[8] This was 1876.

In June of 1908, three Strickland journal entries allude to Mary Louise Strickland's mental condition. The vague examples refer to things she did or said with other people present. "Mr. [William] Lloyd came to see us in the afternoon, and Mrs. S unfortunately had one of her bad turns while he was present and behaved in a way which must have been very embarrassing to him. I have seldom seen her act worse, and he not having been accustomed to such actions on her part was at a loss what to do about it."[9] On the following day, Strickland seemed to note some improvement. "Mrs. S. was in a somewhat saner mood today but is not yet over her paroxysms."[10] During a visit by his cousin Fannie Potter, Strickland noted the effect of her behavior. "Towards evening Mrs S. was much worse than usual and insulted Fannie (if an insane person can be accounted to insult anyone). Fannie received her insults with equanimity she having seen enough before to convince her of the insanity of Mrs. S."[11]

We do not know the exact nature of the woman's medical condition. Her husband believed that she did not want to be examined. "Mrs. S. went to Dr. Parsons who will leave for Europe on the 17th instant, but continued her refusal to submit to an examination."[12] Her condition adds another element of mystery to the couple's troubled relationship. Three months later, Mrs. Strickland did submit to an examination. However, her husband's journal entry fails to define her malady. Dr. Parsons "after an examination of Mrs. S arrived at the general diagnosis that but little could be done in the way of cure and that palliative remedies only were indicated."[13]

Toward the end of 1914, Strickland releases a few more items of information about his wife's condition, evoking elements in her diet and sedentary habits, which may have affected her health. "Mrs. S is not getting on very well, largely I think because she will be imprudent in her diet and in going about more than she should. But then it is I am sure not easy to change the habits of a life-time. She has been accustomed to eat and drink at will and to be about the house at least more or less every day."[14] This is the last note of any length by Mr. S. on Mrs. S.

On New Years Day, 1915, Strickland recorded simply, "Mrs. S. delirious." She died on April 19 of the same year. She was the only member of the family for whom a cause of death was not registered in cemetery records or discernable from journal entries.

Clearly, Peter Strickland spent very little time with Mary Louise outside of the Dorchester home. Whenever he went to visit New London, he went alone or with daughter Mary. Mrs. Strickland rarely took a trip to New London to see her relatives, and when she did, she went alone. In 1910, Peter and Mary Louise continued to write to each other when either went on a solo trip to New London, and they reported on mainly family news. Mrs. Strickland attended church alone. Strickland and his daughter Mary went together to another church. On rare occasions, Mary Louise received visits from her widowed sister Martha. They would go together on outings, such as a trip to Horticultural Hall in Boston.

Inside the home, the parents slept in different rooms, as recorded in Strickland's entry "after calling Sika and her mother who were both fast asleep in their rooms."[15] There is a "black cat" episode.

Strickland writes, "This morning our black cat bit Mrs Strickland on the hand severely and I beat him some for it, a proceeding which he seemed to understand perfectly well."[16] Here Strickland appears solicitous of his wife, but generally he refers to her in very remote terms, as though she were a presence to be tolerated. Significantly, the journal entries covering 1915, the year of her death, are missing; they start again in early 1916. No trace of the husband's emotional loss or mourning can be found.

Since Peter Strickland had spent so much time away from his wife, one may wonder if he had other women in his life. One thinks, in particular, of African women. Capt. Peter Strickland moved to Gorée in 1880 to live in the houses occupied by Capt. Henry O. Skinner since the 1860s. Like Strickland, Skinner was an African agent for the Matthew Bartlett shipping firm of Boston. Skinner had a child with a Senegalese woman.

Skinner and others actually recommended that Strickland take a local woman. Strickland thought little of the idea for at least two reasons: one, it would be costly and two, the situation would leave him open to theft. "I have been advised before now to take a wife wherever I happened to be—even by Skinner—but I tell you what, these improved wives are expensive and they take no interest except in what they can steal."[17]

One also thinks of possible sexual adventures Strickland might have had as a sailor. Strickland writes once about a fellow sailor ill with venereal disease and asks how a man can be so foolish as to contract the disease.

A natural question one asks is: Why did the Stricklands not relocate to New London where they both came from? The family did discuss the possibility. In 1894, from Senegal, Strickland "[W]rote long letters to Mrs S. and to my Daughter Mary, advocating a change to New-London."[18]

The question continued to trouble Strickland more than a decade later after he had resettled in Dorchester.

> My trip to Norwich has made some change in the disposition of my property, and I am reflecting seriously whether it is best for me to make any more changes or not. . . . My cousins, the Comstocks, seem anxious that I shall move with

my family to their vicinity, and personally I am not averse to it. It is not likely however that I shall make any move in that direction at present for the reason that Sika is not in favor of it, and at my time of life I do not wish to make any move which she disapproves of. Left to myself I should probably buy a little farm, fix up the buildings, and move on to it. But I realize that if anything should happen to me that a farm would not be a proper place for my family to live. Farms are all right for families composed of both men and women, but a farm is not a good place for a woman who has to dwell alone.[19]

At this point in his life, Peter Strickland is paying no attention to his wife's desires, only to his daughter's. The daughter has no strong links with New London and may have felt more at home in Boston. From what we detect, the mother may have sorely regretted the move away from her family, yet for whatever reason did not move back to Connecticut.

Peter Strickland makes a comment on women working outside the home, which suggests his unsupportive general attitude. "I am not an enthusiast on the subject of an emancipation for women, which brings them by the wholesale into the industrial market in competition with men. It is not for the best and the world will find it so before the thing goes on much longer. Young women by crowding into positions which were formerly occupied by young men drive the latter away to other countries where they do not meet with the same competition, which in the end works ill for the women."[20]

While Peter Strickland does not sound sympathetic to womankind, his views were typical for his time. On one occasion, he describes a conversation with a doctor showing even less esteem for women. Dr. Bliss was the doctor who cared for the Stricklands' daughter Grace when she had diphtheria. Strickland wrote, "[Dr. Bliss] is not a man morally in whom I have much confidence. . . . I first called on him in 1897, with a view to discuss the mental State of Grace, who was displaying at that time as I thought symtoms [sic] of insanity. I found it impossible to confine him to the subject. He went off on a tirade against women in general, asserting that as a class they were 'curious creatures,' full of whims, caprices, and liable to be affected by hysterics."[21]

Besides considering her insane, Peter Strickland appears to have distanced himself from his wife during her last ten years from 1905 until 1915. He never writes about their doing things together or going out together. During their years in West Africa, father and daughter seem to have bonded into an inseparable unit, leaving Mrs. Strickland in the background when they returned to live with her.

One of Peter Strickland's foremost concerns upon his return from Africa was the need to acquire a cemetery plot for his family. This obsession turned into a project for father and daughter. By 1907, daughter Mary had lost all her three siblings. For the family's final resting place, Strickland unhesitatingly chose the Cedar Grove Cemetery in New London where his ancestors lay. Built in 1851, this cemetery was modeled after the Mount Auburn Cemetery in Cambridge, Massachusetts, which Strickland had visited and admired. Cedar Grove exemplified the rural cemetery movement featuring large tracts of wooded land, in contrast to the smaller church graveyard.

"Went to the Cemetery with Sika, and after looking about in all parts of it, we finally selected lot 46 in section 1st. This lot, 16 X 25 is not far from the middle of the old part of the cemetery. On our arrival at New-London I had the deed for the lot immediately drawn up and drew $500 from the Mariners Savings Bank to pay expenses. I paid $300 for the lot and $100 for perpetual care."[22]

Over the following days, Strickland had the body of daughter Grace transferred from the receiving vault to lot 46, section 1. He wrote his wife a letter from New London giving information on Grace's burial, which Mrs. Strickland did not attend.

Strickland would devote five years, 1907–1912, to planning and establishing the family burial plot at the Cedar Grove Cemetery. Father and daughter spent several days walking around the cemetery and selecting granite stones. Strickland decided upon a large block of the finest granite from Westerly, Rhode Island, with space provided for inscriptions on all sides. Then there were headstones. Peter wanted his older brother Henry, deceased in 1897, disinterred from the Rogers family plot and reinterred in the new plot. This was done. Younger brother Samuel and his wife have their stones in an older part of the cemetery, alongside the father Peter Rogers Strickland (1805–1874) and his wife Laura (1808–1891). The stonemason who carved the inscriptions was a Dutchman, Mr. Hepp, who had a shop near the entrance to the cemetery.

One by one, Strickland sent to Mr. Hepp from Dorchester the inscriptions he had devised for his family members. When it came time to write his own, he was hesitant. "I somehow find it difficult to get at a plan for an inscription on my stone in Cedar Grove Cemetery."[23]

While on visits to New London, Strickland no longer had close family to stay with. He booked accommodations at Mrs. Churchill's rooming house for three dollars a week or at Mrs. Charlotte Graham's on 114 Union St. on the corner of Federal St. He would take meals at Mrs. Holmes'. Strickland kept his New London dentist over the years. Daughter Mary accompanied him to the dental office of Dr. James Linsley on State St. for gold crowns and bridgework. Strickland also entrusted his gold spectacles to Mr. Chidsey to have the lenses changed.

Strickland sometimes hired a two-seated carriage from Buffum's livery stable on the corner of Brainerd and Amity Sts. He loved to drive his daughter around and visit family: Mrs. Fannie Potter, his cousin Nathan Comstock, his grandnephew Charles W. Comstock in Uncasville, and H. R. Douglas.

Soon after Strickland completed writing his own epitaph, he recopied all his personal journals. The retired merchant and consul was clearly preparing for his death and wanted all his papers in order. He explained lapses in writing the journal. "The Book I am now transcribing, begun when I was 19 years of age was the first in which I attempted to keep a Journal and I have kept one off and on ever since. Things have happened at times which made [it] inconvenient, and sometimes my getting out of the habit has made it difficult for me to take up the habit again."[24]

With the family burial plot established, and his journal recopied, Peter Strickland began settling into old age. For several years, however, his retirement had been a physically active one. Behind his house, on one thousand square feet, he practiced the farming skills he had learned from his father. He planted and nurtured Flemish beauty pears; Porter, Baldwin, Hubbardston, and Gravensteen apples; and cherry trees, noting the yield in bushels each year. His vegetable garden, fertilized with horse and cow manure he purchased from a neighbor on Coffey St. included more than a dozen varieties. He summed up his garden philosophy: "On the whole I think a garden in a city is not a paying piece of property, but it serves to give one work in the open which is healthful and elbow-room which is pleasant to have."[25]

Just as Strickland devoted himself to enhancing his garden, so was he a conscientious homeowner. He tended to the repair and maintenance of his two-story frame house on Neponset Avenue: taking off screens, putting on storm windows; ordering coal and stoking the fires in the basement furnace and kitchen stove; and painting the inside and outside of the house, as well as and the fence that surrounded the yard. His stamina appeared to be extraordinary, for he reports at age seventy-three having "[W]orked all day from five in the morning and [to] six at night painting the SE side of the house and accomplished considerable."[26]

In 1911, Strickland fell from a ladder that he had propped against one of his pear trees. He broke no bones but suffered internal injuries that took him several months to get over. He mentions in his journal that daughter Mary cared for him. After the accident, he could never stand up straight. As soon as he was able, however, he returned to such strenuous activities as piling up logs in the cellar for the winter and clearing brown-tail moths from the pear trees. At seventy-four, he finally slowed down. "I felt so fatigued after replenishing the furnace fire in the morning that I sat still in my chair for hours after it."[27] He admits that his greatest regret is that he has not been to church since his fall.

In 1912, Strickland turns seventy-five. His daughter helps him celebrate the day. "This being my 75th birthday Sika made me a present of a nice thermometer to observe the weather with coming winters. She also made a fine cake, and ordered an ice-cream at Billings."[28]

Strickland the neighbor and Strickland the citizen offer two more images of the man. When his property was threatened, Strickland defended himself. He let the authorities know, for example, when he found himself a victim of petty larceny. On June 27, 1911, he addressed a letter to the Superintendent of Police, Fields Corner, Dorchester to report that hoodlums had thrown a large stone at his front door at midnight, and others had robbed his cherry trees of their fruit.[29] A few years later, Strickland "[j]oined with Mr Ward and Mrs Hagamyer in protesting against the noise made by a Goat kept in a vacant lot on Houghton St."[30]

When he went by trolley to Boston, Strickland occasionally stopped in to chat with his former boss, John Frank Brooks, or with another of his shipping masters, Francis C. Butman. Strickland went to visit a former shipmate by the name of Macvey who had become yacht editor of the Boston Herald. He traveled to Brookline to reminisce with William Lloyd, a former shipmate. When Lloyd died in 1911, Strickland wrote movingly,

> I cannot somehow fully realize that my old friend and former shipmate William Lloyd is laying dead at his home in Brookline and that I shall never see him alive in this world again. I was with him in the Bark *Mary E. Dunworth* in I think 1856–7 about ten months. We were common sailors together for about 8 months of the time, and lived in a little room not more than 14 feet long and less than 10 feet in width. There were six of us living in this confined space, which was not much more than enough to meet the requirements of the law in regard to steerage passengers, who only have to endure the discomforts of a sea-voyage for a few days perhaps once in a life-time.[31]

Strickland donated to charities when solicited for contributions, entering in his journal the amount he gave and the name of the recipient institution. For many years, he gave one dollar annually to the Red Cross. To the Salvation Army he donated two dollars. Another institution that sent him a solicitation by mail was the "National Child Labor Committee." Strickland agreed with the cause, to help prevent abuse of children in the labor force. After he sent two dollars to this charity in 1914 he made a tongue-in-cheek entry: "Today I received by mail a letter from the 'National Child Labor Committee' begging me for a Subscription to help forward their cause, and yesterday, when no one was on hand to stop them, a troop of boys came into the yard and after fastening the gate open, shook the nearest pear-tree and carried off from it a large lot of green pears. There are then two sides to the Child Labor Question, for I could heartily wish that the imps which sneak into our yard to steal had something else to do."[32]

Strickland voted for the first time in his life on November 2, 1908. "Hitherto for fifty years I have not been situated so I could exercise the privilege of voting, at least if I happened to be at home on election day I had not had time to examine the measures to be voted on nor the records of the men to be voted for."[33] Strickland voted for the Republican William Howard Taft, and wrote in his journal: "[b]ut I do not consider the issues of such importance that I shall miss any sleep tonight in case [William Jennings] Bryan happens to be elected."[34]

Four years later, Strickland voted for Taft again. He did not care for Theodore Roosevelt, about whom he wrote, "[h]e is something like the character described by Shakespeare who said, 'When I speak let no dog bark.'"[35] In 1912, Strickland voted for Woodrow Wilson.

Besides his exercise of voting privileges, Strickland demonstrated his civic-mindedness in the advocacy of community affairs. In 1911, he wrote to John F. Fitzgerald, mayor of Boston, suggesting a location for a children's playground that the Mayor was espousing. He closed, "All whom I have talked with heartily approve of the location I have mentioned for a playground, and having called the attention of the City to it I will again relapse into the repose which possibly I have earned after serving the interests of Boston for more than half a century mostly in foreign climes. I am esteemed Sir, Very respectfully yours, Peter Strickland."[36] Although Strickland was not known to the Boston elite, he did write letters to important officeholders.

Having lived away from the United States as an adult and voted for the first time at age seventy-one, Strickland did not consider himself attached to one political party. Rather, he saw himself as an internationalist, rare for his epoch. As early as 1876 he wrote: "I hate partisan politics, or partisanship of any kind. I never was cut out for a clique, nor for a sect, nor for a party, not for a nation even, but for the World."[37]

After a long life abroad, Peter Strickland enjoyed the cultural activities that Boston offered. He bought season tickets to the Boston Symphony Orchestra, playing in Symphony Hall, which had opened in 1900: his regular seats were F33 and F34. He sent his daughter to hear Paderewski play the piano in 1907 and again in 1916. He went to hear Serge Rachmaninoff in 1909 conduct his symphonic poem "The Hand of the Dead." In 1910, father and daughter went to the Museum of Fine Arts to admire the Frick collection of paintings. In 1913, he went to see his first moving picture, Victor Hugo's *"Les Misérables,"* which he enjoyed.

In retirement, Strickland continued the lifelong reading habits he had developed as a youth. He became a member of the branch library at Fields Corner, and in 1907–1908 read the *Conquest of Mexico* by Prescott, the *Last of the Mohicans* by Cooper, Stanley's *Dark Continent,* and African travel stories by Mungo Park. His interests focused on literary classics and tales of African exploration and discovery.

Peter Strickland also sought out intellectual stimulation at lectures, often religious in nature, followed by discussions. On Thursdays, he attended meetings of the "Mather Club," held in the parlors of the First Parish Church on Meeting-House Hill. There, on November 4, 1909, he attended a lecture on the topic: "Is Christianity losing its grip on the man who works and thinks?" The same year, he went to King's Chapel to hear Rev. W. W. Fenn, Dean of Harvard Divinity School. He also heard Booker T. Washington describe the workings of Tuskegee Institute.

As a diarist, he noted the major events of the day. Strickland reported on several wars in his long lifetime. His journal contains comments on the American Civil War 1861–1864, the Spanish American War in 1898, the Boer War of 1900, the Russo-Japanese War of 1904, and the First World War 1914–1918. During the Russo-Japanese War, he shared his feelings about war: he predicted that the 1904 war would be the last one. "General Sherman was quite right when he defined war to be Hell, and I think further in the same direction that it is a hellish way of settling difficulties. It is a disgrace to what is called civilization that war among peoples who profess to be civilized is possible, and among the greatest benefactors of their race today are those who are striving against the customs and sentiments of the times to make war impossible. This Century will in all probability see the end of war."[38] Strickland would have been chagrined to learn that a century later the end of war remained elusive.

Strickland closely followed the First World War in the press. On his birthday, August 1, 1914, Strickland found the news from Europe "very disturbing" and "frightful to contemplate." In 1916, he noted that there was a German submarine operating off Nantucket. On April 5, 1917, he confirmed in his journal that Congress had declared war. Peter Strickland and his daughter bought four liberty bonds. When the conflict ended, he perceived one event that symbolized the world's returning to normalcy: "The news came that Yale beat Harvard by one-half a length in the [crew] race yesterday at New London which shows that things are settling down again to normal."[39] The war over, Strickland expressed enthusiasm for the League of Nations, as proposed by President Woodrow Wilson.

Strickland noted early air travel in the United States, and in particular one air show with acrobatics. "There was much passing of automobiles, carriages, electric cars and even of people on foot toward Quincy and Squantum in the early part of the day and in the evening a procession equally great passed in the opposite direction. Those who went to Quincy had the pleasure of witnessing the launch of what is called the largest war-ship in the world, the Argentine battleship *Rivadavia*, and those who went to Squantum saw several air-ships of different kinds whose aviators were trying to out-do each other in their maneuvers."[40]

Strickland never owned a motor vehicle. However, he did enjoy taking a rare trip in an automobile. He would refer to the coming of the automobile and the disappearance of the carriage, or the sleigh in winter, as a mark of the times he lived in. He also recognized the passing of the age of sail. "We are hearing now for the first time this winter Sleigh-bells, but the automobiles in diminishing the number of horses have decreased also the number of people who own sleighs. . . it is possible that the sleigh as well as other pleasant things we were once accustomed to will eventually meet the fate of the sailing-ship."[41]

Another new feature of Strickland's life was piped-in water. In 1907, he mailed a letter to the Luckett-Wake Company, which supplied West Africa with leaf tobacco, in which he wrote: "The plumber came . . . . my family would think it strange now if they were obliged to get their water from an icy well the same as we had to once."[42]

His journal contains information on the cost of everyday living, with his comments thereon. In 1912, with butter at almost fifty cents a pound and eggs at thirty cents a dozen, he considered the price of these items "too dear to use lavishly."[43] When he took a pair of shoes to Thayer & McNeil to be resoled and reheeled in 1918, he duly noted the price he paid, $2.75.[44] For a shave, Strickland paid fifteen cents. While he did not indicate the cost, he bought the albums in which he wrote his journal at Hooper, Lewis & Co. Blank Book Manufacturers Stationers & Importers of English & French Stationery and Fancy Goods, 120 and 122 State St., Boston or at Aaron R. Gay & Co., Stationers, also at 122 State St., Boston. He left his razors and scissors to be ground at Codman & Shurtleffs.

To a former business partner in Senegal, he offered comparative figures: "The price of labor in America at the present time is probably double what it is in Europe. I have been making repairs in my house of late for which I had to pay carpenters 55 cents an hour, masons 65 cents, plumbers the same."[45]

As a lifelong writer, Peter Strickland penned newspaper and magazine articles from home and submitted them for publication. He often voiced his disappointment at the decline of American shipping and trading around the world. In one letter to a friend in 1911, he focused his attention first on Boston harbor, and then on the sad state of American shipping in general.

> It is a matter of note that an interest is being awakened in the Dock system of Boston, which it is said is not now adequate to accommodate the Commerce that Boston considering its happy position as a sea-port has a right in the future to expect. The fact has indeed been commented on that Boston is not keeping pace with Baltimore and other coastal cities south and west of it in developing its capabilities as a commercial emporium, and a sentiment seems to be growing among Bostonians that no time should be lost in remedying this state of things. Reciprocity with Canada will doubtless have

some tendency to attract the winter trade of that vast and productive region towards its convenient and ice-free port, so that on the whole there seems to be justification for the proposal to spend a large amount of money in improving its docks so that the very largest ships may find ample accommodations in Boston's beautiful harbour. It is not a pleasing thought however that the most of the ships to be accommodated will not fly the America's flag, were not built in American ship-yards: are neither manned nor owned by Americans, and have no interests here whatever save the all-pervading one of self-interest.[46]

Flag displays were an idiosyncratic symbol of Strickland's allegiances. Having spent most of his adult life in a French colony, the consul had become quite attached to France. Displaying the French flag was a habit he had developed in Senegal. He once told a visitor how his own small sailing craft could be recognized: "it's the boat with the American flag under the French flag." In Dorchester, he wrote at age eighty: "We took in our American & French flags which had been displayed in honor of its being the French National holiday."[47] On Aug. 6, Lafayette's birthday, he displayed both French and American flags, acknowledging French help at the time of the American Revolution. He would fly the American flag on Independence Day, Christmas, and Easter. On Good Friday, it was his custom to fly the flag at half-mast.

In retirement and far from West Africa, Peter Strickland loved to receive mail from his former neighbors and colleagues in Senegal. For over a decade, he kept up correspondence with them. He wrote especially to the neighbor across the alley, Claude Potin, and congratulated him upon becoming mayor of Gorée in 1916. He corresponded with Alexandre Desproges, the postmaster of Gorée and with the mayor of Rufisque, Gabriel Escarpit. He followed the news of the new railroad line between Dakar and Kayes. When Senegal had a good agricultural season, he was informed. Strickland was not surprised to hear that the governor-general of French West Africa left his mansion on Gorée and moved into his new palace in Dakar on July 14, 1907.

For a researcher looking into the Strickland papers a century later, one correspondence is frustrating: mention of enclosures exchanged between Claude Potin and Peter Strickland. A 1909 letter to Potin thanks him for the pictures he had sent to Dorchester. In return, Strickland enclosed eight photographs of Boston scenes plus a photograph Mary took of the Strickland house and their newly purchased rental property next door. Both sets of photographs seem to have disappeared.

The purchase of the Neponset Avenue house in 1870 and of the next-door residence in 1908 for rental income provided the family with financial security up until daughter Mary's death in 1945. Peter Strickland worked hard for sixty years, from age fifteen to age seventy-five. He received a moderate stream of income during the long period he worked in the merchant marine and African trade. He earned only a small income as a consul through the fees he collected; he received no pension from the State Department when he retired.

Always aware of the purchasing power of the dollar or of the franc, Strickland realized that in retirement he had to be careful of his spending. "Spent a part of the day in going over my accounts, and it almost frightens me to note the present cost of things. If interest had kept at 6% as it used to be, and had the cost of living not advanced I could live comfortably now, but with interest low and lowering and the cost of living 25% more than it used to be, we as a family shall have to practice the strictest economy in order to live."[48] In retirement, his annual income from all sources was around $2,000, supporting a family of three and then two. In 1907, he expressed his financial situation in maritime terms: "On account of the funds which I have received from Africa since I left there I have been enabled to avoid going astern much."[49]

About this same time, Strickland realized that the purchase of the house next door, 96 Neponset Avenue, could be a sound investment. Referred to in county records as the house of Joseph T. Orne, the one and one-half-story frame house with six rooms and bath stood on 10,000 square feet of land. The owner at the time, Elmira L. Park, and her daughter, Mrs. Hume, went over to the Strickland house on November 25, 1908, and agreed upon a sale price of $3,150. The following year, Strickland rented out 96 Neponset Avenue for $18 a month.

102 Neponset Avenue, the two-story frame house with seven

rooms and a bath plus a two-story storehouse that Strickland had purchased from Harriet W. Burditt on Aug. 26, 1870, stood on 7,600 square feet of land. During his retirement, taxes on this house and on the rental property next door cost Strickland about $100 a year.

For a few years around 1900, Peter Strickland held two other rental properties in nearby Massachusetts towns: on 11 Foster Street in Everett and on 7 Basket Street in West Roxbury. His annual mortgage payments for each were $1,000. One Roxbury property sold at a loss to Strickland of $100. The documentation on the Everett house is complicated: it includes a twenty-one-page letter by Mary Strickland to the family of a Mr. Carter who she claims owed her father $1,000. The outcome of the Everett house rental is unclear, but evidently not to Strickland's financial advantage.

Strickland made one known stock investment, suggested by a grand nephew. In 1903, Charles W. Comstock sent Strickland a prospectus on a new electric railway to be laid between New London and Westerly, Rhode Island.[50] Peter signed up for twenty shares of stock and his daughter Mary bought ten shares in the Uncas Power Company.[51]

Another contribution to the Strickland family's financial security was a bequest of over five thousand dollars from Peter's father, kept in two New London banks. Strickland found it handy to make small withdrawals during his numerous visits to that city during his adult life. Mary also used these funds after her father died.

Peter Strickland's will, drawn up in Suffolk County, Boston, on July 6, 1921, left no debts and a balance of $9,261.22 in his personal estate. This sum was divided as follows:[52]

Table 6. Assets in Strickland Will

Boston, Mass. bank account	$ 287.33
New London, Conn. bank account	7,772.94
Norwich, Conn. bank account	1,000.95
Furniture and household effects	200.00
Uncas Power Company	"Value doubtful"
Total	$9,261.22

As for Strickland's real estate, his 102 Neponset Avenue house was valued at $3,500 and his 96 Neponset Avenue house at $3,000. The grand total of personal and real estate came to $15,761.22.

The father had chosen his daughter Mary, the last surviving child, as the executrix and beneficiary of his will. Her mother had died in 1915. Mary Strickland continued to live in the 102 Neponset Ave. house and kept the rental property next door until she died in 1945. Then the two properties were sold for $6,600 and $4,000, respectively. Mary had bank accounts in Boston and New London, and some jewelry to her name. Mary never received an income of her own, but appears to have lived on the rental income plus savings left by her father.

For eight years, the retired Strickland maintained his contacts with the Tennessee-based tobacco company he had represented in Senegal. He received a commission for assisting and advising Luckett-Wake on tobacco sales to the French business community in Senegal. He translated some French documents for them. He received tobacco samples from Tennessee, which he sent to the French company headquarters in Bordeaux along with explanations in French. Strickland penned a courteous and moving letter to the widow of the patriarch of the Luckett-Wake Company in 1913. "We have received the sad news of the death of your noble and widely-esteemed husband, F. D. Luckett, Esq. . . . My relations with your husband were always pleasant, and I think that he made everyone who had dealings with him feel that they might trust him implicitly. He possessed in a high degree the best instincts of the Southern Gentleman."[53]

Following Luckett's death, all accounts between Strickland and Luckett-Wake were settled. Strickland reflected on the end of their business dealings.

> It seems to me decidedly queer not to be connected in any manner with business. Since I was in my "teens," I have had work almost continually, so that it has seemed to be a part of my nature to be connected with it, and I have now got no particular work or business to think of. But I am 75 years of age, and have perhaps done my share of the "World's Work," although I have a feeling and am glad that I have got

it that I should be willing to do more if I am given strength and opportunity as perhaps I shall be. I have still enough to do about the house; in fact I cannot get time to accomplish all I should like to of such work; but this seems too much connected with my daily routine of living to afford me entire satisfaction. One hardly likes to feel that he has no longer anything to do in the world except to exist and to give all his attention to those wants of his nature connected with existence. One still longs to do something which shall count for the world, and I think the most of those who have generous natures manage to make themselves useful in some manner clear through to the end.[54]

Strickland had once described a day of retirement in these terms: "spent the day existing." In summing up his life and contributions, let us note that the man constantly tried to accomplish not only mundane tasks but also "something which shall count for the world." He did not derive satisfaction from mere existence.
Strickland's last journal entry was on Sunday, June 1, 1921. In a shaky hand, he scratched in the barometer reading of the day, "1930," and then put down his pen. Once more, he would lift it up: on July 6, to sign his last will and testament. When Peter Strickland died at his Dorchester home on November 13, 1921, there was little mention of his passing: only a two-line obituary in the *Dorchester Beacon* and a five-line obituary in *The Day* from New London. A eulogy was pronounced at the gravesite at the Cedar Grove Cemetery in New London, but the text has not been saved. Strickland's recognition would come not at his death, but through the discovery of his written legacy. Captain Strickland is buried between two other New London shipmasters, Nathanial Middleton and William Baker. Fittingly, Peter Strickland lies next to an octogenarian like himself on one side, and on the other, a youngster who perished at sea like his son George.

8

Summary and Conclusions

Homeward Bound

We are lucky that Peter Strickland lived to tell the tale of his long, productive life. He survived close calls at sea, including one where his vessel was dismasted near the spot where the *Titanic* went down. He managed to escape death during the cholera and yellow fever epidemics that sent so many Europeans in West Africa to the White Man's Grave.

Teacher, sailor, author, merchant, and consul: we admire Peter Strickland for the variety of worthy activities he mastered over a lifetime. We marvel at the smooth transition from his maritime experience to a business career, leading directly to his consular appointment. He was simultaneously an author and a sailor. He served as consul while pursuing his commercial interests. Indefatigable diarist, he wrote a daily journal over a sixty-four-year period during which he moved from one vessel to another, one continent to another, one profession to another, all the while observing and noting how the world was evolving and how he viewed changing events.

Peter Strickland deserved more recognition than he received. As the only American who worked forty years in the import-export sector in West Africa over the period 1864–1905, he became an expert in transatlantic commerce. His maritime expertise was earned through nearly fifty years of active service in several classes of sailing vessels on many seas. His consular career of over two decades in French West Africa made Strickland a pioneer who left behind a substantial record of his activities. Stuart Kennedy reminds us that consular contributions habitually get short shrift. "Because the diplomatic work of the Foreign Service has been looked upon as more prestigious, the contributions of consuls in diplomatic history have been virtually ignored."[1]

Strickland endured disappointments and great sorrows. He received only meager fees, but never a salary for his work as consul. Three of his children predeceased him, including his son George, who might have carried on Peter's work and name. Strickland survived these blows and lived his life with energy, religious faith, idealism, and a strong work ethic. He accumulated a store of knowledge on marine, diplomatic, and business subjects, and had the intelligence and creativity to manage his affairs effectively. He endeavored to contribute to the world until the end of his long life.

One of Strickland's deepest cares was to improve the condition of sailors. He would have to wait until 1915 and the passage of the "Seaman's Act" to see appreciable improvement both in the lot of sailors and in the safety of maritime travel. Robert La Follette, the progressive Wisconsin Senator, championed this legislation designed to give rights to the merchant marine similar to those already won by American factory workers. In particular, the Act established the right of crews to sue for damages against negligent ship owners, it limited working hours to nine-hour days, and it guaranteed minimum standards of cleanliness and safety. Strickland's pleading for amelioration in the sailor's condition was written forty years before the enactment of La Follette's legislation. Regretting that sailors enjoyed no lobby in Congress, Strickland would no doubt have rejoiced that legislation finally protected their interests.

Diplomatic historians will place Strickland's consular dispatches in the rich context of his business correspondence plus his daily journal written in West Africa, where Strickland was expected to cover an immense and little-known territory by himself. Rarely has a consul reported so prolifically on an area over such an extended period. Strickland's reports on the epidemics and quarantines were circulated by the State Department, anxious to protect American seamen and passengers in the region. The department obviously appreciated all the special consular reports Strickland sent, as it forwarded them to other agencies for publication. Today's diplomats will be appalled to learn of the State Department's failure to provide for a diligent consul overseas for twenty-three years, and will shake their heads over the long and unresolved controversy between the two parties over his salary.

Strickland would be worthy of study simply for his amazing feat of keeping a journal over a sixty-four-year period—let alone his other deeds and legacies. While his 2,000 letters are informative, his 2,500 pages of journal are frank and spontaneous. The neat, readable, recopied albums begin in the voice of a nostalgic teenaged sailor who misses his mother in Connecticut. They end in the weary tones of an old man—tired, bent, and ill—who has buried a wife and three children and written his own epitaph.

Strickland's journal permits us not only to look at events and decisions but also to understand how Strickland perceived them. We find evidence that at several times in his career Strickland grappled with uncertainty. An introspective man, he mused on the consequences of his actions and speculated on what might have happened to him. On a few occasions, he vowed not to embark on a specific course of action, only to do exactly that at a later date.

In the journal pages for 1864, we find several such allusions to contingencies in Strickland's life. In March, he wrote, "If it had not been for the loss of the fore-finger of my right hand when I was about sixteen by a felon, I should probably now be in the navy."[2] Strickland was feeling sorry for himself searching for a berth during the Civil War and realizing the dangers of being at sea during that time. However, he imagined that his life as a navy sailor "on board of a river craft gunboat" could have been worse.

In June 1864 Matthew Bartlett's representative in Gorée sized up Strickland as a candidate to buy and sell for the company up and down the West African coast. Strickland found two reasons not to accept: "For me, I do not think I would like such a position, because it would not only be dangerous for my health but keep me away from home."[3] Nevertheless, despite his initial strong reservations on two separate counts, he eventually took the traveling position.

In July 1864, Strickland debated whether to go home to see his family after a trip to Africa or to look for another berth. "Shall I go home when the vessel gets to Boston or not? This is a question, which occupies my attention now to the exclusion of many others. If I go home I shall lose much time and it will cost a good deal but if I do not go I shall miss seeing those I love and it is possible [I'll] never have the chance again. I think I shall be apt to go, and not violate a rule I once made to see my mother every chance I could which I have hitherto kept pretty well."[4]

In this case, Strickland's hesitation worked out to his advantage. Rather than hurrying home, he remained around the vessel in Boston for several days, getting to know its owner, Matthew Bartlett, during his daily visits to the craft. Impressed by Strickland's conscientiousness, Bartlett gave him several days off to see his family in New London without removing him from the payroll.

In October 1864, Strickland is under consideration to become Matthew Bartlett's representative in Gorée, succeeding Captain Henry Skinner. Strickland confides in his journal, "I know that I am wanted to take his place but think I shall decline absolutely if the position is offered to me, no matter what the consequences may be."[5] Despite his initially recoiling from the idea, Strickland eventually takes the Gorée-based job.

The person that Strickland grew closest to was his daughter Mary. One of the last insightful quotations from his journal, three years before his death, focuses on his relationship to family and the future. Prompted by his wedding anniversary, sober thoughts occurred to Capt. Peter Strickland at his twilight in life. His wife had died three years before.

> This being the 57th anniversary of my Wedding day, my mind has been considerably occupied since in the course of my domestic life and I find that just now I am not ideally situated. I find that although I have a home for the moment I have not an heir and no prospect of one and that the prospect of a happy future for the only child I have left who has been an object of my constant care for years is not of the best. If we were settled in or about New London where some people at least know of us things should be some better, but with no relative within a hundred miles and no influential acquaintance to turn to in case of emergency when friends are required the prospect for my poor daughter ahead certainly looks sobering.[6]

Strickland again is debating whether moving back to New London would make sense. Mrs. Strickland had also equivocated for a long period on whether she should move back to New London or stay in Boston where she must have felt isolated and friendless. Strickland actually interrogated one of Mary's unmarried cousins in New London to see if she would welcome Mary to join her in New London on a permanent basis. The suggestion was not favorably received.

The last years of the Peter Strickland family are cloaked in mystery just as some aspects of Peter Strickland's existence were. Although Strickland mentions keeping a daily journal most of his life, the known volumes cover only twenty-five years out of the sixty-four-year span. In particular, the period covering the seventeen months before and after his wife's death, February 1, 1915, until June 30, 1916, is totally missing. In the volumes that exist, over one hundred pages have been ripped out.

Some day, more information on Strickland's life may surface. We can be thankful that four archival collections, in Delaware, Connecticut, and Maryland in the United States and Dakar in Senegal, contain significant original material by Strickland. The views of someone other than the principal protagonist would be helpful additions to the Strickland record. Nevertheless, we are grateful for Strickland's commitment to his daily journal and determination to preserve his writings.

It is from this journal that we select a final quotation where a sea captain aged twenty-seven projects a time in the distant future when he will reflect on his life.

Lat 41º.20′ N. Long 68º.33′ W. There has not been much change in the wind or the weather and the sea is decidedly smoother. We are now near Georges Shoal and in sounding got 25 fathoms of water.

One month ago today I left my home in New London to go I then knew not whither but I now find it was for Africa. It does not seem so long but time in certain circumstances flies very quickly. To look ahead, a lifetime seems a long period and in some cases it may no doubt seem long. But if I am permitted to live to old age, and look back on my lifetime as I do now and in the same light I shall no doubt think it has been short. I shall think how "like a hurried dream" it has all been.[7]

Epilogue

August 10, 1983 marked an important day in the relations between Senegal and the United States. When American President Ronald Reagan spoke to reporters at the South Portico of the White House, he began with these remarks: "It's been an honor and a pleasure to welcome President Abdou Diouf to the White House today. And it is especially fitting that our meeting takes place on the 100th anniversary of our American consulate on the Senegalese island of Gorée." Peter Strickland would have been surprised and pleased to know that a President of the United States a century later would refer to the consulate he opened.

Strickland would have been even more astonished to learn that an American president had actually honored the same consulate with his visit. In March 1998, President Bill Clinton became the first sitting American president to visit Senegal. The last event in his schedule was an address before a large crowd on the island of Gorée. Prior to stepping up to the podium near the low, round fort in Gorée harbor, Clinton entered a courtyard, resplendent with pink bougainvillea, yellow laurel, and red hibiscus. This location served as a "holding station," where the president could relax a bit and, if he cared to, spend a moment going over the speech he was about to deliver. At his side was Abdou Diouf, still President of Senegal fifteen years after his visit to the Reagan White House. A photograph on the back cover of this book shows the presidential pair being welcomed into the former home of Capt. Peter Strickland in Senegal.

Notes

Most of the notes derive from three sources:
(A) the Peter Strickland Manuscript Collection no. 69, Mystic Seaport Library, Mystic, Conn.;
(B) the Peter Strickland Papers, University of Delaware Library, Newark, Del.; and
(C) State Department documents at the National Archives and Records Administration (NARA) in College Park, Maryland.

A few references are drawn from the National Archives in Dakar, Senegal. The collection in Mystic is comprised of 12 volumes. Delaware arranges its collection into 15 folders. In each case, the documents are arranged in chronological order in bound albums. The State Department's consular files consulted at NARA are from Record Groups (RG) 59 and 84. Below, the word "dispatch" refers to the consular reports Strickland sent to the State Department which are part of RG 59 at NARA. The references to "Journal" and "Letter to" signify the journal of Peter Strickland and a letter written by Peter Strickland.

Preface

1. J. Gérard Bosio, Michel Renaudeau, *Souvenirs du Sénégal* (Dakar: Visiafric, 1980 vol. 1; 1983 vol. 2).
2. Department of State, U.S. National Archives and Records Administration (NARA) Record Group 59, microfilm file T573, "Dispatches from U.S. Consul in Gorée-Dakar, French West Africa, 1883–1906."
3. Albert Nelson Marquis, ed., *Who's Who in New England* (Chicago: A.N. Marquis & Company, 1909), 900.
4. *The National Cyclopaedia of American Biography* (New York: James T. White Co., 1899), 9:503.
5. Capt. P. Strickland, *A Voice from the Deep* (Boston: A. Williams & Co., 1873).
6. Letter to John F. Brooks, Mar. 30, 1881. Delaware folder 13.

7. Journal, Aug. 12, 1898. Mystic vol. 13.
8. Letter to Frank W. Woodward of Boston, Mar. 25, 1898. Mystic vol. 13.

Chapter 1 – Child of New London

1. Frances Manwaring Caulkins, *History of New London, Connecticut from the first survey of the coast in 1612, to 1852*, 2nd edition. (New London: published by the author, 1860), 259-266.
2. Ipswich quarterly court records of Essex County, Mass. vol. 4, 121.
3. Camille Hanlon, *Dissenters and Community Builders: The Rogers and Bolles Families in Early New London* (Unpublished manuscript in the Charles E. Shain Library, Connecticut College, New London, 1996).
4. The tender teaching age of fifteen may surprise. Nevertheless, Calvin Coolidge states in his autobiography that he passed the qualifying exam to teach in Vermont at age thirteen. In the president's family, that was not a record: his sister Abbie taught school at age twelve.
5. Journal, June 15, 1864. Delaware folder 3.
6. Journal, Nov. 5, 1860. Delaware folder 2.
7. Letter to George Strickland, Oct. 22, 1876. Delaware folder 8.
8. Journal, June 12, 1907. Mystic vol. 6.
9. Journal, Sept. 21, 1912. Mystic vol. 8.
10. Journal, Jan. 2, 1859. Delaware folder 2.
11. Journal, May 2, 1909. Mystic vol. 6.
12. Journal, Aug. 11, 1862. Delaware folder 2.
13. In old English, a felon is an abscess or an infection.
14. Journal, Mar. 29, 1864. Delaware folder 3.
15. Journal, Feb. 20, 1864. Delaware folder 3.

Chapter 2 – Sailor on the Atlantic

1. "Cyclopedia," a fifty-four-page album of miscellany into which Peter Strickland copied disparate entries covering the period 1852–1913. Delaware folder 7:30.
2. Journal, Mar. 2, 1857. Delaware folder 1.
3. Journal, Dec. 6, 1863. Delaware folder 2.
4. Letter to Dean Wood, Oct. 2, 1902. Delaware folder 9.
5. Journal, Jan. 4, 1857. Delaware folder 1.
6. Journal, Dec. 23, 1876. Delaware folder 5.
7. Journal, Aug. 8, 1864. Delaware folder 3.
8. Letter to Matthew Bartlett, Apr. 10, 1878. Delaware folder 8.
9. Letter to Matthew Bartlett, Oct. 15, 1879. Delaware folder 8.

10. Journal, July 24, 1859. Delaware folder 2.
11. Journal, Dec. 25, 1860. Delaware folder 2.
12. Journal, Mar. 23, 1859. Delaware folder 2.
13. Journal, Aug. 3, 1860. Delaware folder 2.
14. Journal, Apr. 25, 1861. Delaware folder 2.
15. Journal, Mar. 14, 1857. Delaware folder 1.
16. Journal, Dec. 12, 1857. Delaware folder 1.
17. Journal, Apr. 30, 1857. Delaware folder 1.
18. Journal, June 27, 1857. Delaware folder 1.
19. Journal, Jan. 25, 1860. Delaware folder 2.
20. Journal, Feb. 1, 1861. Delaware folder 2.
21. Journal, Apr. 28, 1861. Delaware folder 2.
22. Journal, Oct. 29, 1862. Delaware folder 2.
23. Journal, Nov. 7–26, 1863. Delaware folder 2.
24. Journal, Jan. 8, 1864. Delaware folder 3.
25. Journal, Apr. 21, 1864. Delaware folder 3.
26. Journal, Oct. 17, 1864. Delaware folder 3.
27. "Journal from Boston towards Gorée." Mystic vol. 1.
28. Journal, Sept. 4, 1865. Mystic vol. 1.
29. Journal, Oct. 25, 1862. Delaware folder 2.
30. Journal, Apr. 4, 1857. Delaware folder 1.
31. Journal, Mar. 20, 1859. Delaware folder 2.
32. Journal, Jan. 26, 1864. Delaware folder 3.
33. Journal, Dec. 25, 1857. Delaware folder 1.
34. Journal, Aug. 28, 1904. Delaware folder 6.
35. Journal, Nov. 14, 1864. Delaware folder 3.
36. Letter to Laura Strickland, Oct. 1, 1876. Delaware folder 8.
37. Letter to George Strickland, Nov. 26, 1876. Delaware folder 8.
38. Journal, Jan. 13, 1894. Mystic vol. 5.
39. Journal, Sept. 6, 1916. Mystic vol. 9.
40. Letter to *Boston Transcript*, Aug. 12, 1898. Mystic vol. 13.
41. Letter to *Boston Transcript*, Aug. 26, 1898. Mystic vol. 13.
42. Journal, Apr. 16, 1912. Mystic vol. 8.
43. Journal, Dec. 25, 1859. Delaware folder 2.

Chapter 3 – Author from Boston

1. Dispatch 111, Aug. 10, 1889.
2. Journal, Jan. 28, 1912. Mystic vol. 8.
3. See illustration, page 106.
4. Strickland, *Voice*, 7.
5. Ibid., 9–10.

6. Ibid., 61.
7. Ibid., 65–66.
8. Ibid., 61.
9. Ibid., 40.
10. Ibid., 63.
11. Ibid., 73.
12. Ibid., 76.
13. Ibid., 88.
14. Ibid., 102.
15. Ibid., 122–124.
16. Ibid., 113.
17. Ibid., 132.
18. Ibid., 133.
19. Ibid., 134–35.
20. Ibid., 161–162.
21. Ibid., 182.

Chapter 4 – Merchant in West Africa

1. Letter from Samuel Swan to James Andrews, Jan. 20, 1816, in the Peabody Essex Museum, Salem, Mass. as quoted in Norman R. Bennett & George E. Brooks Jr., *New England merchants in Africa: a history through documents, 1802–1865*. Boston: Boston University Press, 1965, 79.
2. From the George Howland voyage to West Africa 1828–1829, manuscript in the Rhode Island Historical Society, quoted in Bennett & Brooks, *New England merchants*, 146.
3. Journal, Mar. 29, 1861. Delaware folder 2.
4. Letter to Frank Potter, Apr. 17, 1880. Delaware folder 13.
5. Letter to Claude Potin, June 22, 1903, Delaware folder 12.
6. Letter to Harper & Bros., Nov. 1, 1902. Delaware folder 9.
7. Letter to Harper & Bros., Apr. 17, 1885. Delaware folder 11.
8. Letter to Director of the Interior, French Government, St. Louis, Senegal, June 17, 1890. Mystic vol. 11.
9. Letter to Dr. & Mme. Primet, Mar. 19, 1897. Mystic vol. 11.
10. Kennedy, *American Consul*, 146.
11. Letter to Benjamin Potin, Aug. 24, 1903. Delaware folder 12.
12. Letter to W. T. Grant, Aug. 26, 1903. Delaware folder 12.
13. Letter to Luckett-Wake Tobacco Co., Sept. 15, 1903. Delaware folder 12.
14. Letter to Macleod Reid & Co., Sept. 15, 1903. Delaware folder 12.
15. Letter to Benjamin Potin, Sept. 28, 1903. Delaware folder 12.
16. Letter to Macleod Reid & Co., Sept. 28, 1903. Delaware folder 12.

17. Letter to Benjamin Potin, Sept. 28, 1903. Delaware folder 12.
18. Letter to Claude Potin, Jan. 22, 1908. Delaware folder 10.
19. Letter to Maurel & Frères, June 5, 1911. Delaware folder 10.
20. M. Laurent, «*Le tabac dans les colonies*» in J. Charles-Roux, *Exposition Universelle de Paris 1900: Les colonies françaises et pays de protectorat* (Paris: Ministère des colonies, 1900), 628–638.
21. NARA RG 84, vol. 11.
22. NARA RG 84, vol. 11.
23. Maine, New York, and Massachusetts led the United States in shipping natural ice. More than a million tons were shipped in a year. Although ice exports began as early as 1820, the glory years were 1870–1900.
24. Journal, July 12, 1864. Delaware folder 3.
25. Department of State, NARA RG 84, vols. 10–11. In the few instances where Consul Strickland neglected to record the date when or place where a vessel was built, the Mystic Seaport Library's digital Ship and Yacht Registers database supplied the figures.
26. The three anomalies consist of (A) an 1886 voyage of the bark *Beatrice Havener* taking coal from Cardiff, Wales to Gorée-Dakar and then going in ballast to Barbadoes; (B) the schooner *Spring-Bird* having brought salt to Gorée-Dakar from Cape Verde Islands traveled in ballast to the Isle of May, Scotland in 1886; and (C) the schooner *David A. Story* bringing fruit from Cape Verde Islands to Gorée-Dakar in 1902 and going in ballast to the Isle of May, Scotland.
27. NARA RG 84, vols. 11–12.
28. Joseph B. Hoyt, "Salem's West Africa Trade 1835–1863 and Captain Victor Francis Debaker," Essex Institute Historical Collections Vol. CII (1966), 37–73. Hoyt explains that Salem's Africa trade—mainly with the Gold Coast (now Ghana)—was its last maritime gasp. "Why the Africa trade died is fairly clear. The death of the ship owners, the lack of local markets, the rise of Boston markets, the increasing difficulty of using Salem harbor, and transportation problem all were factors."
29. Strickland Notes, Delaware folder 7, 112.

Chapter 5 – Resident on Gorée Island

1. From notes at the *Institut fondamental d'Afrique Noire* on Gorée left by Belgian archeologist Guy Thilmans who conducted research in Senegal from 1965 to 2001.
2. Journal, Nov. 5, 1864, Delaware folder 3.
3. National Archives, Dakar, Senegal, file 3 G 2/133.
4. Journal, Apr. 15, 1897. Mystic vol. 5.
5. Journal, July 26, 1894. Mystic vol. 5.

6. Journal, Mar. 18, 1905. Delaware folder 6.
7. Journal, Mar. 24, 1905. Delaware folder 6.
8. Journal, May 14, 1895. Mystic vol. 5.
9. Journal, Jan. 10, 1895. Mystic vol. 5.
10. Journal, May 10, 1904. Delaware folder 6.
11. Journal, Mar. 20, 1905. Delaware folder 6.
12. By "tow-babs," Strickland is referring to the expression in the West African market language "bambara" used to designate persons with white skin. It is usually written "toubab."
13. Letter to Mrs. Francis Lawton, Jan. 12, 1896. Mystic vol. 11.
14. Journal, May 24, 1894. Mystic vol. 5.
15. Journal, Jan. 9, 1904. Delaware folder 6.
16. Journal, Mar. 5, 1904. Delaware folder 6.
17. Journal, Sept. 29, 1895. Mystic vol. 5.
18. Journal, Nov. 30, 1895. Mystic vol. 5.
19. Letter to Dr. Metin, Feb. 15, 1897. Mystic vol. 11.
20. Letter to Dean Wood, Aug. 21, 1902. Delaware folder 9.
21. Letter to Xavier Boyer, June 7, 1902. Delaware folder 9.
22. Letter to Dr. & Mme. Metin, Dec. 25, 1897. Mystic vol. 11.
23. Journal May 3, 1904. Delaware folder 6.
24. Journal, Jan. 5, 1905. Delaware folder 6.
25. Journal, Feb. 26, 1905. Delaware folder 6.
26. Journal, June 27, 1904. Delaware folder 6.
27. Journal, Mar. 15, 1904. Delaware folder 6.
28. *Journal Officiel*, Nov. 12, 1904. Delaware folder 14.
29. Journal, Feb. 2, 1904. Delaware folder 6.
30. Letter to Claude Potin, July 8, 1910. Delaware folder 10.
31. Dispatch 251, Mar. 28, 1904.
32. National Archives, Dakar, Senegal, file 3 G 2/105.
33. Journal, Mar. 20, 1904. Delaware folder 6.
34. Journal, Apr. 3, 1904. Delaware folder 6.
35. Journal, Apr. 21, 1905. Delaware folder 6.
36. Letter to Claude Potin, Jan. 15, 1907. Delaware folder 10.
37. Letter to Macleod Reid & Co., Jan. 26, 1899. Mystic vol. 14.
38. Letter to Dr. & Mme. Metin, Sept. 17, 1899. Mystic vol. 11.
39. Journal, Apr. 14, 1896. Mystic vol. 5.
40. Journal, Mar. 14, 1896. Mystic vol. 5.
41. Letter to Mrs. Francis Lawton, July 3, 1898. Mystic vol. 11.
42. Journal, Aug. 9, 1904. Delaware folder 6.
43. Journal, May 18, 1905. Delaware folder 6.
44. National Archives, Dakar, Senegal, file 3 G 2/133.

Chapter 6 – Consul to Senegal

1. Charles Stuart Kennedy, *The American Consul: A History of the United States Consular Service, 1776–1914* (New York: Greenwood Press, 1989), 9.
2. Kennedy, *American Consul*, 146.
3. Cooper to Lyons 1826–1827; Hawthorne to Liverpool 1853–1857; Howells to Venice 1861–1865, and Harte to Glasgow 1880–1885.
4. Dispatch 31, July 13, 1885.
5. Department of State, U.S. National Archives and Records Administration (NARA) Record Group 84, US Consulate at Gorée-Dakar, 1883–1905. vol. 13, Apr. 26, 1895.
6. NARA Record Group 59, microfilm file T573.
7. Kennedy, *American Consul*, 128.
8. Regulations prescribed for the use of the Consular Service of the United States (Washington, DC: Government Printing Office, 1881), 3.
9. Dispatch 16, Oct. 22, 1884.
10. Published consular reports are accessible through US Congress Session, House Miscellaneous Documents, Congressional Information Service, US Serial Set Index.
11. Dispatch 53, Nov. 4, 1886.
12. Dispatch 145, Sept. 30, 1891.
13. Dispatch 205, June 28, 1898.
14. Dispatch 222, Feb. 8, 1901.
15. Dispatch 253, May 13, 1904.
16. Dispatches 260–263 of Nov. 12–Dec. 22, 1904.
17. Dispatch 235, Oct. 15, 1902.
18. NARA RG 59, microfilm file T573, undated State Department note appearing among 1904 dispatches from Strickland.
19. Dispatch 251, Mar. 28, 1904.
20. Dispatch 87, Apr. 5, 1888.
21. Dispatch 57, Jan. 18, 1887.
22. Dispatch 38, Mar. 30, 1886.
23. Dispatch 189, Nov. 18, 1895.
24. Dispatch 20, Jan. 24, 1885.
25. NARA RG 59, microfilm file T573, telegram, July 22, 1893.
26. Dispatch 5, Feb. 2, 1884.
27. Dispatch 140, June 6, 1891.
28. Dispatch 12, July 19, 1884.
29. Dispatch 150, Feb. 3, 1892.
30. Dispatch 183, Apr. 27, 1895.
31. National Archives, Dakar, Senegal, file 3 G 2/105.

32. Dispatch 184, June 6, 1895.
33. Dispatch 208, Mar. 20, 1899.
34. Dispatch 221, Jan. 24, 1901.
35. NARA RG 84, vol. 6, State message no. 84 to Strickland, Apr. 15, 1897.
36. Dispatch 256, Aug. 18, 1904.
37. National Archives, Dakar, Senegal, file 10 F 5.
38. Letter no. 446 from the lieutenant governor of Senegal, referred to in Strickland undated letter of appreciation to the lieutenant governor in NARA RG 84, 5:13.
39. National Archives, Dakar, Senegal, file 10 F 5.
40. Dispatch 14, Aug. 29, 1884.
41. Dispatch 221, Jan. 24, 1901.
42. NARA RG 84, vol. 6.
43. Dispatch 269, June 23, 1905.
44. Dispatch 31, July 13, 1885.
45. Letter to Dean Wood, Oct. 2, 1902. Delaware folder 9.
46. Photocopy of the letter provided to the author by the Quincy Historical Society, Adams Academy Building, Quincy, Massachusetts.
47. Dispatch 83, Feb. 20, 1888.
48. NARA RG 84, vol. 6.
49. NARA RG 84, vol. 15.
50. Dispatch 108, June 3, 1889.
51. Letter to Assistant Secretary of State, Oct. 2, 1897.
52. NARA RG 84, vol. 6, Oct. 8 1897.
53. NARA RG 84, vol. 6, State Department message no. 30 to Strickland, July 11, 1887.
54. Dispatch 197, Jan. 17, 1897.
55. Dispatch 38, Mar. 30, 1886.
56. Dispatch 87, Apr. 28, 1888.
57. Dispatch 135, Jan. 22, 1891.
58. Dispatch 143, Sept. 18, 1891.
59. Dispatch 149, Jan. 9, 1892.
60. Dispatch 169, July 24, 1893.
61. Dispatch 177, Jan. 1, 1894.
62. Dispatch 196, Nov. 17, 1896.
63. Dispatch 198, Mar. 22, 1897.
64. Dispatch 203, Jan. 13, 1898.
65. NARA RG 59, microfilm file T573, State Department Consular Bureau internal memo, Mar. 7, 1903.
66. Dispatch 267, May 27, 1905.
67. NARA RG 59, microfilm file T573, telegram from State Department, June 23, 1905.

68. Dispatch 272, Oct. 28, 1905.
69. NARA RG 59, microfilm file T573, letter to State Department, June 21, 1906.

Chapter 7 – Retiree in Dorchester

1. Three years before the *Titanic*, the RMS *Republic* of the same White Star Line also sank. The ship went down on Jan. 24, 1909, off Nantucket, Massachusetts after a collision with another vessel.
2. Letter to Claude Potin, Oct. 4, 1905. Mystic vol. 15.
3. Journal, Aug. 29, 1904. Delaware folder 6.
4. Letter to Claude Potin, Jan. 15, 1907. Mystic vol. 11.
5. Letter to Gabriel Escarpit, Jan. 15, 1907. Mystic vol. 11.
6. Journal, Dec. 24, 1863. Delaware folder 2.
7. Letter to Dr. Metin, Mar. 25, 1900. Mystic vol. 11.
8. Journal, Oct. 9, 1876. Delaware folder 8.
9. Journal, June 10, 1908. Mystic vol. 6.
10. Journal, June 11, 1908. Mystic vol. 6.
11. Journal, June 21, 1908. Mystic vol. 6.
12. Journal, June 10, 1914. Mystic vol. 8.
13. Journal, Sept. 10, 1914. Mystic vol. 8.
14. Journal, Nov. 30, 1914. Mystic vol. 8.
15. Journal, Apr. 5, 1913, Mystic vol. 8.
16. Journal, Nov. 29, 1912. Mystic vol. 8.
17. Letter to Matthew Bartlett, Aug. 30, 1879. Delaware folder 8.
18. Journal, Nov. 18, 1894. Mystic vol. 5.
19. Journal, Feb. 9, 1907. Mystic vol. 6.
20. Journal, Feb. 28, 1907. Mystic vol. 6.
21. Journal, Jan. 8, 1907. Mystic vol. 6.
22. Journal, June 3, 1907. Mystic vol. 6.
23. Journal, Feb. 8, 1913. Mystic vol. 8.
24. Journal, Feb. 20, 1913. Mystic vol. 8.
25. Journal, Aug. 24, 1911. Mystic vol. 7.
26. Journal, June 22, 1910. Mystic vol. 7.
27. Journal, Jan. 3, 1912. Mystic vol. 8.
28. Journal, Aug. 1, 1912. Mystic vol. 8.
29. Letter to Dorchester Superintendent of Police, June 27, 1911. Delaware folder 10.
30. Journal, June 28, 1917. Mystic vol. 9.
31. Journal, July 24, 1911. Mystic vol. 7.
32. Journal, July 28, 1914. Mystic vol. 8.
33. Journal, Oct. 14, 1908. Mystic vol. 6.

34. Journal, Nov. 3, 1908. Mystic vol. 6.
35. Journal, June 11, 1910. Mystic vol. 7.
36. Letter to Mr. Fitzgerald, Mar. 28, 1911. Delaware folder 10.
37. Journal, Oct. 8, 1876. Delaware folder 8.
38. Journal, Nov. 5, 1904. Delaware folder 6.
39. Journal, June 21, 1919. Mystic vol. 10.
40. Journal, Aug. 26, 1911. Mystic vol. 7.
41. Journal, Dec. 28, 1909. Mystic vol. 7.
42. Journal, Jan. 14, 1907. Mystic vol. 6.
43. Journal, Feb. 29, 1912. Mystic vol. 8.
44. Journal, July 6, 1918. Mystic vol. 9.
45. Letter to Fernand Calcat, Nov. 18, 1907. Delaware folder 10.
46. Undated insert after letter to Frank Woodward, July 14, 1911. Delaware folder 10.
47. Journal, July 14, 1917. Mystic vol. 9.
48. Journal, Mar. 6, 1907. Mystic vol. 6.
49. Journal, June 29, 1907. Mystic vol. 6.
50. Letter to Charles W. Comstock, Sept. 18, 1903. Delaware folder 12.
51. Journal, Feb. 20, 1907. Mystic vol. 6.
52. Letter to Mrs. F. D. Luckett, June 2, 1913. Mystic vol. 11.
53. Journal, Jan. 10, 1913. Mystic vol. 8.

Chapter 8 – Summary and Conclusions

1. Kennedy, *American Consul*, vii–viii.
2. Journal, Mar. 29, 1864. Delaware folder 3.
3. Journal, June 12, 1864. Delaware folder 3.
4. Journal, July 2, 1864. Delaware folder 3.
5. Journal, Oct. 17, 1864. Delaware folder 3.
6. Journal, June 11, 1918. Mystic vol. 9.
7. Journal, April 16, 1864. Delaware folder 3.

Peter Strickland Genealogy

First generation
Peter Strickland (c1646–c1722)
Of British descent. Having lived in Massachusetts, the first Peter
Strickland died in New London, Connecticut.

Fifth generation
Peter Rogers Strickland (1805–74), farmer,
married Laura White (1808–91) in 1827 in New London.

Children:
Mary Anne (1827–32)
Henry Rogers (1830–97)
Peter (1837–1921)
Samuel William (1841–1901).

Sixth generation
Peter Strickland (1837–1921), sailor,
married Mary Louise Rogers (1832–1915) in 1861 in New London

Children:
Peter (1862–63)
George (1864–88)
Mary (1868–1945)
Grace (1875–1906)

No issue from the sailor's children.

Peter Strickland Chronology

1837	Born in New London, Connecticut
1852	Teaches school, leaves home for a seafaring life
1856	Second mate on merchant sailing ship
1860	Chief mate on merchant sailing ship
1863	Captain on merchant sailing ship
1864	First merchant voyage to West Africa
1864–82	Agent for Boston shipping house of Matthew Bartlett
1871	Purchases home in Dorchester, Massachusetts
1873	Publishes book *A Voice from the Deep*
1876–79	Based in Bissau (Portuguese Guinea) in West Africa trade
1880–1905	Based on Gorée (in French colony of Senegal) in West Africa trade
1883–84	Agent for Boston shipping house of F. C. Butman
1883	Named U.S. consul to Gorée-Dakar by President Chester Arthur
1883	Arrives in Senegal and opens first American consulate
1888–1916	Agent for Luckett-Wake Tobacco Co. of Clarksville, Tennessee
1905	Relinquishes consul position in Senegal and leaves Africa
1906	Retires in Dorchester from the U.S. consular service
1921	Dies in Dorchester, buried in New London.

Bibliography

Andrews, Scott. "The Last Best Ice." *Portland [Maine] Winter Guide* 7, no. 10, 1992.

Atlas Universel d'Histoire et de Géographie. Paris: L. Hachette, 1865.

Baker, Henry A. *History of Montville, Connecticut, formerly the North Parish of New London, from 1640 to 1896*. Hartford: Case, Lockwood & Brainard Co. Press, 1896.

Barry, Boubacar. *Senegambia and the Atlantic Slave Trade*. Cambridge: Cambridge University Press, 1988.

Bell, R. C., ed. *Diaries from the Days of Sail*. New York: Holt, Rinehart and Winston, 1974.

Bennett, Norman R. and George E. Brooks Jr. *New England Merchants in Africa: A History through Documents, 1802–1865*. Boston: Boston University Press, 1965.

Brooks, George E. Jr. *The Kru Mariner in the Nineteenth Century: An Historical Compendium*. Newark, Del.: Liberian Studies Association in America, 1972.

Brooks, George E. Jr. *Yankee Traders, Old Coasters, & African Middlemen*. Boston: Boston University Press, 1970.

Caulkins, Frances Manwaring. *History of New London, Connecticut from the First Survey of the Coast in 1612, to 1852*, 2nd ed. New London: published by the author, 1860.

Coe, Harrie B., ed. *Maine–A History*, vol. 3. New York: Lewis Historical Publishing Co, 1928.

Comstock, Cyrus B. ed. *A Comstock Genealogy: Descendants of William Comstock of New London Who Died after 1662*. New York: Knickerbocker Press, 1907.

Comstock, John Adams. *A History and Genealogy of the Comstock Family in America*. Los Angeles: Commonwealth Press, 1949.

Decker, Robert Owen. *The Whaling City: A History of New London*. New London: New London County Historical Society, 1976.

Foote, Andrew H. *Africa and the American Flag*. New York: D. Appleton, 1854. Reprint, New York: Negro Universities Press, 1969.

Genealogical and Biographical Record of New London County, Connecticut. Chicago: J. H. Bears, 1905.

Grant, Stephen. "Capt. Peter Strickland and Dorchester, 1864–1921." Dorchester, Mass.: Dorchester Historical Society, Dorchester Historical Society Occasional Pamphlet, 2004, 1–23.

_____. "Captain Peter Strickland of New England: Trader and Consul in West Africa, 1964–1905." *Sea History* (Peekskill, N.Y.) 114, Spring 2006, 32–35.

_____. "*Le drapeau américain sur l'île de Gorée: l'histoire de Peter Strickland, premier consul américain au Sénégal*." American Center Information Bulletin, U.S. Embassy, Senegal No. 42, March 2004, 1–4.

_____. "Peter Strickland: Sea Captain from New London, First U.S. Consul to French West Africa, Agent in Transatlantic Trade." *Collections* XI (University of Delaware Library), 2003, 82–106.

_____. "Capt. Peter Strickland (1837–1921) of New London." New London: New London County Historical Society Newsletter, Nov.–Dec., 2002, 3–4.

Hanlon, Camille. *Dissenters and Community Builders: The Rogers and Bolles Families in Early New London*. Unpublished manuscript in the Charles E. Shain Library, Connecticut College, New London, 1996.

Hare, William E. II, ed. *Greetings from New London, Connecticut: a Collection of Early 20th Century Post Cards*. New London: New London County Historical Society, 1991.

Heidler, David S. & Jeanne T. eds. *Encyclopedia of the American Civil War*. Santa Barbara: ABC-Clio, 2000.

Hempstead, Joshua. *Diary of Joshua Hempstead, 1711–1758*. Collections, vol. 1. New London: New London County Historical Society, 1901.

Hoyt, Joseph B. "Salem's West Africa Trade 1835–1863 and Captain Victor Francis Debaker." Salem, Mass.: *Essex Institute Historical Collections* 102, 1966.

Jones, Chester Lloyd. *The Consular Service of the United States, its History and Activities*. Philadelphia: Published for the University of Pennsylvania, 1906.

Kennedy, Charles Stuart. *The American Consul: A History of the United States Consular Service, 1776–1914*. New York: Greenwood Press, 1989.

Klein, Martin A. *Slavery and Colonial Rule in French West Africa*. Cambridge: Cambridge University Press, 1998.

Lagrillière-Beauclerc, Eugène (chambres de commerce du nord). *Mission au Sénégal et au Soudan; voyage d'André Lebon, ministre des colonies, 1897*. Paris: Tallandier, 1898.

Laurent, M. "Le tabac dans les colonies" in J. Charles-Roux, *Exposition Universelle de Paris 1900: Les colonies françaises et pays de protectorat*. Paris: Ministère des colonies, 1900, 628–638.

Lengyel, Emil. *Dakar: Outpost of two hemispheres*. New York: Random House, 1941.

Marfaing, Laurence. *L'Evolution du Commerce au Sénégal 1820–1930*. Paris: Harmattan, 1991.

National Archives, College Park, Md. Dispatches from U.S. Consul in Gorée-Dakar, French West Africa, 1883–1906. Record Group 59, microfilm file T573; Record Group 84.

National Archives, Dakar, Senegal. Files 3 G 2/105; 3 G 2/133; 10 F 5.

National Cyclopaedia of American Biography. New York: James T. White & Co., 1899.

Nelson, Harold D., et al. *Area Handbook for Senegal*. 2nd ed. Washington, D.C.: U.S. Government Printing Office, 1974.

Orcutt, William Dana. *Good Old Dorchester: A Narrative History of the Town 1630–1893*. Cambridge, Mass.: Published by the author, 1893. Reprint by Heritage Books, Bowie, Md., 2002.

Peter Strickland Manuscript Collection 69, Mystic Seaport Library, Mystic, Conn.

Peter Strickland Papers, University of Delaware Library, Newark, Del.

Rogers, James Swift. *James Rogers of New London Connecticut, and his Descendents*. Boston: The Compiler, 1902.

Rogers, John G. *Origins of Sea Terms*. Boston: Mystic Seaport Museum, 1985.

Rosengarten, Theodore. *Tombee, Portrait of a Cotton Planter, with the Journal of Thomas B. Chaplin (1822–1890)*. New York: William Morrow, 1986.

Ruddy, John J. *Reinventing New London*. Charleston: Arcadia, 2000.

Stein, Douglas L. *American Maritime Documents 1776–1860 Illustrated and Described*. Mystic, Conn.: Mystic Seaport Museum, 1992.

Stiller, Jesse H. *George S. Messersmith: Diplomat of Democracy*. Chapel Hill: University of North Carolina Press, 1987.

Strickland, Jim & Dolores. *Descendants of Peter Strickland* (Family tree). Oxnard, CA. Unpublished manuscript, 2006.

Strickland, Mary. Will. No. 324806, Commonwealth of Massachusetts, Suffolk County, Aug. 21, 1945.

Strickland, Peter. "How American Trade in West Africa is Handicapped." Department of Commerce & Labor, U.S. Bureau of Statistics, U.S. Bureau of Manufacture. Consular Reports, no. 289, 1904, 70–72.

_____. "Need of Direct Steamship Service to Africa." Department of Commerce & Labor, U.S. Bureau of Statistics, U.S. Bureau of Manufacture. Consular Reports, no. 257, 1902, 141–149.

_____. "Tariff Changes and Trade in Senegal." Department of Commerce & Labor, U.S. Bureau of Foreign Commerce, U.S. Bureau of Manufacture. Consular Reports, no. 128, 1891, 16–19.

_____. *A Voice from the Deep*. Boston: A Williams & Co., 1873.

_____. Will. No. 200238, Commonwealth of Massachusetts, Suffolk County, Dec. 8, 1921.

Tyng, Charles. *Before the Wind, Memoir of an American Sea Captain, 1808–1833*. New York: Penguin, 1999.

Wadleigh, Wells Eggleston. *Cedar Grove Cemetery, 1851–1976*. New London: New London Cemetery Association, 1976.

About the Author

Son of a book publisher, Stephen Grant was born in Boston. Both his parents were Connecticut bred. He graduated from Amherst College and earned a doctorate in education at the University of Massachusetts.

Serving for over 25 years as Foreign Service officer with the United States Agency for International Development, Grant lived in Ivory Coast, Guinea, Egypt, Indonesia, and El Salvador. He spent seventeen years of his professional life in West Africa, where he managed USAID assistance projects designed to improve local educational systems.

One feature which attracted the author to the idea of writing a biography of Capt. Peter Strickland was the opportunity it offered to revisit Massachusetts, Connecticut, and West Africa. While the parallel is not total, the author and subject inherited or adopted the same triangular geography during their lives. While in their twenties, they discovered West Africa. For one, the region was in the early stages of colonization; for the other, the early stages of independence. The State Department sent both of them to French-speaking areas of West Africa on long-term assignment.

Grant is the author of three volumes based on old picture postcards. In three developing countries where he worked—Guinea (1991), Indonesia (1995), and El Salvador (1999)—he commercially published books linking vintage photography to social history. His investigative techniques included archival research, visits to cemeteries, and interviews with old-timers.

Indices

Bold indicates illustration

People Index

Abercrombie, George   85
Alexander II, czar of Russia   23
Angrand, Léopold Armand   87,
   92–93, 96, 132
Armand, Charles   127, 133
Arthur, Chester   118, 188

Baker, William, Capt.   14, 20, 166
Bartlett, Matthew   17–18, 27–28,
   30, 66–67, 70, 78, 82, 86, **105**, 133,
   152, 171–72, 188
Basse, Marie   88
Blaine, James G.   119
Boyer, Xavier   87, 92–93, 182
Brito, Antonio, Capt.   **109**, 117, 129
Brooks, John Frank   71–72, 82, 157
Burditt, Harriet W.   164
Butman, Francis C.   67, 73, 82, 95,
   127–29, 136, 157, 188
Butman, Frank R.   95

Calcat, Fernand   186
Chase, H. H., Capt.   130
Cleveland, Grover   118
Clinton, Bill   175
Clinton, George, Sir   96–97, **108**
Comstock, Asa   33–34, 152

Comstock, Charles W.   33–34, 152,
   155, 164
Comstock, Elizabeth   33–34, 152,
   223
Comstock, Nathan   33–34, 36, 152,
   155
Comstock, Zebediah   33–34, 152
Cooper, James Fenimore   115, 159
Correa, Antoine   88
Cromie, Captain   91

Da Silva, Carlo   87–88
Da Silva, Luiz   88
Deloncle, Captain   38
De Ruyter, Michiel, Admiral   85
Desproges, Alexandre   95, 162
Desproges, Amélie   95
Dior, Lat, king of Cayor   121
Diouf, Abdou   175
Diouf, Marie   88
Douglas, H. R.   155

Escarpit, Gabriel   148, 162
Everett, William   133–34

Fall, Marie-Anne   88
Fanning, Happy Lavinia   35
Fellows, Adeline   36
Fitzgerald, John F.   158
Fortier, Edouard   97, **108**

Graham, Charlotte   155
Grant, Ulysses S.   115
Guiraud, Jean   98
Guy, Camille   131

Harrison, Benjamin   81, 118
Harte, Bret   115
Hawthorne, Nathaniel   145
Hay, John   119
Howe(s), Captain   50
Howells, William Dean   115
Howland, George, Capt.   65

La Follette, Robert   170
Lawton, Francis   182
Lee, J. Beveridge, Rev.   xxv
Lincoln, Abraham   25
Linsley, James, Dr.   155
Lloyd, William   18, 150, 157
Luckett, F. D.   70–72, 165

Maclean, Colonel   91
McDonald, Captain   17
McKinley, William   118–19
Middleton, Nathaniel, Capt.   166

N'Jean, Marie   89, 118

Park, Elmira L.   163
Potin, Benjamin   180–81
Potin, Claude   67, 72, 94, 98–99,
    148, 162–63, 181–82, 185
Potin, François   94
Potin, Louis   94
Potin, René   94–95, 138
Potter, Fannie   150, 155

Reagan, Ronald   175
Rogers, Benjamin N.   136
Rogers, Charles   5
Rogers, Martha Washington   9,
    149

Rogers, Mary Louise (Mrs. S)   xx,
    111, 134, 148–54, 172–73, 187
Rogers, Orlando   8
Rogers, Tommy   10
Roosevelt, Theodore   118, 158
Root, Elihu   119
Roume, Ernest   96, 98, **108**

Sagna, Marie-Therese   88
Seck, Charles   117
Shaw, Captain   27
Silverzweig, Benjamin   8, 37
Silverzweig, Bertha   37
Skinner, Henry O., Capt.   27, 30,
    86, 152, 172
Sprague, Horatio Jones   119
Strickland, George   xx, **47,** 70, 95,
    102, **112,** 119, 129, 133–38, 149,
    166, 170, 178–79, 187
Strickland, Grace   134, 148–49,
    153–54, 187
Strickland, Laura White   33, 35,
    155, 187
Strickland, Mary (Sika)   xx–xxi,
    xxiv, 6–8, 88–91, 96, 102, 119,
    127, 134, 147, 149, 151–56, 163–
    65, 172, 187
Strickland, Peter Rogers   xxiii, 3,
    155, 187
Strickland, Henry Rogers   4–5, 8,
    149, 154, 187
Strickland, Samuel White   4–5,
    155, 187

Taft, William Howard   158
Taylor, Edward Thompson, Rev.
    51
Texier, Captain   101
Thilmans, Guy   181

Washington, Booker T.   159
Watlington, Benjamin, Capt.   14

Wilson, Woodrow   158, 160
Wood, Dean   178, 182, 184
Woodward, Frank   178, 186

Yerby, William James   142

Place Index
Algiers   116
Argentina   33
  Buenos Aires   33
Atlantic   xix, xxv, 3, 14, 17, 27, 34,
  36–38, 65–66, 75–76, 169

Belgium   98
Bermuda   26
(Guinea) Bissau   19, 32, 118, 123,
  131, 136, 149, 188
  Bissau   5, 34, 66, 77, 79, 87, 95,
  99, 116, 118, 136, 149, 150, 188
  Bulama   49, 90
  Cacheu   66
Britain   97–98
  England   3, 25, 30, 45, 69, 137,
  141
    Liverpool   14, 72, 147
    London   97, 171

California   5
Cape Hatteras   26
Cape Town   116
Cape Verde Islands   4, 28–29, 32,
  77, 79, 87, **109**, 116–18, 128–30,
  134, 136, 140
  Brava   118
  Fogo   32
  Sal   118
  Santiago   116, 118, 128
  San Vicente   118
Colombia   131
Connecticut   3–5, 10, 14, 28, 78–79,
  100, 133, 153, 171, 173, 187–88

Chapel Hill   6
Chesterfield   4–6, 8, 10
  Walnut Hill   8
  Cohansic   6
Connecticut College   35
Dolbeare Hill   6
East Lyme   3–4
Long Island Sound   8
Montville   3–5, 7–8, **111**
Mystic   vii–ix, xxi, 177–78, 180–
  82, 185–86
Mystic Seaport   vi–ix, xiii, xxi,
  xxiv, 28, 70, 177
  New London   3–9, 14–15, 28,
  31, **41**, 82, 100, **111–12**, 133,
  136, 138, 148–49, 151– 55, 160,
  164–66, 172–73, 187–88
    County Historical Society
    189-90
    First Baptist Church   8
    First Congregational Church
    9
  Norwich   152
  Palmerstown   8
  Uncasville   8, 155
Copenhagen   19

Dahomey (Benin)   123
Delaware   xxiv, 173, 177–82,
  184–86
  University of Delaware at
  Newark   vi, xiii, xxi, xxiv, 173,
  177

France   33, 68, 73, 97–99, 115–16,
  121, 126, 133, 162
  Bordeaux   **44**, 67, 69, 71, 76, 116,
  147, 164
  Boulogne   116
  La Rochelle   116
  Le Havre   116
  Lyons   116

Marseilles   76, 87, 116, 129
Nantes   116
Nice   116
Paris   **44**, 73, 91, 95, 100, 115–16, 123, 131, 135, 137
French West Africa (*Afrique Occidentale Française* or *AOF*)   **108**, **110–12**, 116, 123, 131, 138, 142, 162, 169, 188

Gabon   116
(The) Gambia   66, 79, 96–97, **108**, 120, 122, 140
Bathurst   77, 79, 96–97, 116–18, 132, 136, 140
Germany   23, 98
Hamburg   22–23
Ghana (Gold Coast)   17
Guinea   xvii
Conakry   131
Rio Nuñez   32, 66, 79, 118, 136

Havana   26, 31

Italy   98
Ivory Coast   17, 123, 192

Kentucky   70, 73, 95, 100
Louisville   70, 100

Liberia   116, 130–31, 137
Luanda   116

Madagascar   116
Maine   76, 78–79
Kennebec River   76
Portland   76
Massachusetts   xxii, xxiv, 3, 4, 6, 18, 38, 82, 91, 99, 108–9, 154, 164, 187–88
Boston   8, 15, 17, 19, 22, 26–28, 30–31, 35, 39, **44–46**, 51, 57–58,

66–68, 70, 73, 75, 78–79, 82, 91, 95, 100, **105**, **111**, 117–18, 126–30, 133, 136–38, 141–42, 147, 149, 151–53, 157–59, 161–65, 171–73
Boston Museum of Fine Arts   159
Boston Symphony Orchestra   159
Brookline   18, 157
Dorchester   6, 38, **42**, 52, 70–72, 91, 134, 147–52, 154–55, 157, 162–63, 166, 188
Fields Corner   157, 159
First Parish Church   159
Historical Society   189
Mather Club   159
Meeting-House Hill   159
Medford   65
Nantucket   160
New Bedford   4, 8, 79, 130
Mauritania   123
Mauritius   116
Mexico   22, 32, **45**
Veracruz   22, 32

New England   8, 35, 79, 82
Newfoundland   38
New Orleans   5, 15, 26, 33
New York   6–7, 14, 25, **41**, 78–79
Brooklyn   17–18
New Amsterdam   85
New York City   17–18, 68, 79, 85, 126

Niger   120, 123, 127
Nova Scotia   37
Sable Island   37

Panama   **110**, 131
Portugal   99, 117

Rhode Island   25, 30, 65, 79, 154, 164

Providence   9, 26, 65, 79
Westerly   154, 164

Senegal   4, 8, 27, 29, 32, 65–67,
    70–73, 76–79, 82, 85–86, 88,
    90–91, 94, 96, 99–101, **104–5, 107,**
    109–10, 115–127, 130–32, 134,
    136, 138–39, 142, 147, 150, 152,
    161–62, 165, 173, 175, 188
Bakel   121
Cape Manuel   29
Cape Verde Peninsula   102, 129
Dakar   32, 67–68, 78, 86–88, 91,
    93, 95–98, 100–102, 117, 121–25,
    127, 131, 135–37, 141, 143, 147,
    162, 173
Gorée (Goree)   27–31, 42, **43–44,**
    46, 65, 67–69, 71–73, 78–79,
    85–89, 91–103, **104–7,** 118,
    120–23, 125, 127, 131, 133–35,
    138, 142–43, 147–48, 152, 162,
    171–72, 175, 188
Gorée-Dakar   68, 73, 75–77, 79,
    82, 115, 118, 120, 124–25, 127,
    130, 136, 139–140, 142, 188
Rufisque (Rifisk)   31–32, 67, 77,
    79, 87, 98, 118, 120, 125, 147,
    162
Saint-Louis (St. Louis)   29–31,
    67, 69, 77, 79, 91, 118, 122–23,
    131, 134–36, 138, 147
Senegal River   29, 118–21
Seychelles   116
Sierra Leone   77, 79, 116–19, 125,
    132, 140, 142
Freetown   140
Soudan (Mali)   123
Spain   98, 122
Madrid   15
Stockholm   33

Tangier   116

Tennessee   68, 70, 73, 142, 165, 188
Clarksville   68, 70, 188
Memphis   142
Texas   5
Terrel   5
Tripoli   116
Tunis   116

Uruguay   98, 132
Montevideo   22, 25

Virginia   10
Alexandria   10

Washington, D.C.   15, 52, 116–17,
    119, 123, 127, 137, 140–42, 159
West Africa   4–5, 17, 27–28, 30, 32–
    33, 39, 46, 52, 66, 67, 70–72, 77,
    79, 82, 85, 97, **105, 110,** 116, 120,
    126, 131–32, 136, 140, 148–49,
    150, 154, 161–62, 169–71, 192
West Indies   5, 79
Nassau   15

Zanzibar   116

Vessel Index

Alabama   26
Albert L. Butler   80
Alice   80–81
Angola   40
Annanwilde   80
Annie Fairfax   80
Annie L. Palmer   81
Argus   65
Arlington   80, 118
Arthur Egglers   40
Atlantique   40
Auburndale   80
Avala   40

Beatrice Havener   81

Belle Bartlett   81
Belmont   80
Benjamin Willis   15, 40
Bourgogne   37–38
Bruce Hawkins   81

Candace   40
Caroline   13
Charles A. Sparks   81
Charles F. Ward   40, 80
Charles H. Fabens   81
Charles William   13
Chicopee   40
Chili   40
Clara L. Sparks   80
Clotilda   13
Clotilde   80
Colonel Slatterly   13
Colorado   80–81
Compliance   13
Congo   40
Cordillère   40, 147
Cromartyshire   37
Crotoni   25

D. Godfrey   18
Dahomey   97
Daisy   81
Daniel Webster   40
David A. Small   80–81
David A. Story   81
Dido   13

E. H. Yarrington   40
Edith   80
Elm   40
Elsie Fay   80
Ethan Allen   26

Falcon   13
Fannie A. Spurling   80
F. C. Clark   13

Federal   65
Freeman   80

Galena   13
Gazelle   40
General Scott   80

Hancock   80
Hattie & Lottie   80
H. C. Sibley   80
H. E. Thompson   40, 81
H. E. Willard   81
Herald of the Morning   40, 81
Hiram Emery   80
Horace   13
Humphrey Purinton   40
Hydrangea   27, 40

Ida Blanche   40
Indian Queen   17, 28, **46**, 147
Inlian   13

James B. Jordan   81
Jeanette Waemann   40
Jeanne Lippitt   40, 80
Jennie Cushman   40, 73, 75–76, 80, 128
Jennie Diverty   40
J. H. Ward   40
John H. Pearson   80
John M. Ball   81
John Smith   81
John Swan   81
José Oliveira   81
Justin H. Ingersoll   81

Kaluna   81

Laconia   13
Ladoga   13
Lamoine   80
Lancaster   40

Lavinia F. Warren   81
Leon S. Swift   80–81
Leonora   81
Levi S. Andrews   40, 81
Lily   101–2
Longwood   80
Lorenzo   13
Lucy C. Snow   40, 80, 127
Lula E. Wilbur   80

Magdala   13
Magellan   33, 98
M. E. Higgins   40, **47**, 80, 118, 129,
    134, 136, 138
Mariner   13
Martha L. Thomas   81
Mary Allerton   40
Mary A. Clark   81
Mary E. Dunworth   13–14, 20, 23,
    157
Mary Joof   40
Mayflower   40
Megunticook   40, 80
Motley   76, 81
Moustique   102

Nantais   102
Nantasket   80
Nellie May   81
New England   40
New Hampshire   13
New World   13
New York   13
Normandie   40

Oliver Cromwell   40, 80, 130
Onolaska   80
Oriental   13
Oxnard   13

Perseverance   13

Rapid   40
Rebecca Goddard   80
Rebecca L. Evans   40, 80, **109**, 117,
    129
Republic   40, 147
Rhone   13
Richard Alsop   40
Ripple   40, 80, 127
Rivadavia   160
Robert Wing   27–31, 36, 40, **46**, 78
Ruth   82, 81

S. G. Haskell   81
Saphir   101–2
Sarah Jane   40
St. Croix   80
Screamer   81
Scythia   40
Seth Sprague   13
Spring-Bird   80–81
Sullivan   40, 80

Timothy Field   80
Titanic   36, 38, 169
Tranquebar   13
Tremont   40, 80
T. V. C. Hawes   78, 80
T. W. Dunn   81

Unique   40, 81

Waldemar   40
Warren Hellett   40
White Cap   80
Wide Awake   80
Willard Mudgett   80
William A. Ellis   13
William E. Terry   80
Willie G.   81

Zingarella   15, 17, 40, **105**, 150

General Index

American Tobacco Company   71

Assemat, L. Frères   67

Berlin Conference (1883)   121

Boarding-masters   54

Boston Transcript   37

Buhan L. E. père fils   67

Catarrh   34

Cedar Grove Cemetery   154–55, 166

Chavanel, E.   67

Chesapeake and Ohio Railway
   Company   70

Cholera   127, 169

Civil War   9, 17, 25, 27, 33, 159,
   171

Compagnie Française de l'Afrique
   Occidentale (CFAO)   **63**, 72,
   129

Congress   56, 115, 141, 160, 170

Consul   15, 39, **42–43**, **47**, 52, 54–
   55, 65–69, 72–73, 76–79, 82, 86,
   91–92, 94–95, 97–100, 102, **110–
   12**, 115–22, 124, 127–35, 137–42,
   148, 155, 162–63, 169–70, 188

Consulate   68, 73, 92, 95, 97, **107–
   9**, **112,** 115–16, 118–19, 124–25,
   129, 132–33, 137–42, 148–49, 175,
   188

Day, The of New London   100

Delmas, A. & Clastres   67

Department of State (State Department)   51–52, **83**, 95, **107**,
   115–16, 118–19, 121–22, 124,
   127–28, 130–35, 137–38, 140, 142,
   163, 170

Department of Treasury (Treasury
   Department)   117, 132

Devès & Chaumet   67

Entente Cordiale (1904)   97

First World War (World War I)
   159–60

Foreign Service   116, 169

Grant, W. T.   70–72

Gum   31, 65, 67, 76, **105**, 121

Harpers Bazar   100

Harpers Weekly   100

Hides   27, 30, 33–34, 65, **75–78**,
   105, 128, 136

Ice (harvested)   76

Journal Officiel   98, 100

Kru (Kroo, Krou)   17–19

Louisville Courier-Journal   70, 100

Luckett-Wake Tobacco Company
   6, 68, 70–2, 95, 142, 160, 165, 188

Lumber   27, 65, **74**, 78, 92, 136

Macleod Reid & Co.   72

Malaria   32, 67, 127, 133, 150

Maurel & Frères   67, 72, 92, 104,
   147

Maurel & Prom, H.   67

Maurer, A.   67

McKinley tariff   126–27

Mount Auburn Cemetery   154

North American Review   130

Offret, E.A.   67

Peanuts   27, 29–31, 34, 67, 76–78,
   126

Privateer   8, 15, 25–26

Russo-Japanese War (1904)   122–23, 159
Sabbath   7, 22, 56
Seaman's Act   170
Seamen's Friend Society   57
Ship owner   26–28, 30, 53–54, 66, 67, 70, 73, 77, **105**, 133, 170
Shipping agent   54, 58, 126
Slave trade   86
Slavery   4, 23–25, 55, 61
Smallpox   32, 137
Smithsonian Institution   100
Spanish-American War (1898)   122, 159

Teisseire, A.   67
Tobacco   27–28, 30, 65, 70–73, **74**–75, 78, 86–88, 100, **105**, 126, 130, 136, 161, 165

Tobacco trust   71
Treaty of Vienna   85
Typhoid   32, 127

UNESCO   85

Vézia & Cie   67
Voice from the Deep, A   16, 51–52, 188

War risk   26
Who's Who   5
Williams, A. & Co.   51
World Exposition of 1900   73

Yellow fever   67, 89, 96, 127, 137, 140, 169

www.ingramcontent.com/pod-product-compliance
Lightning Source LLC
Chambersburg PA
CBHW031506270326
41930CB00006B/275